# The Howard and Haymes Family Trees

## The story of two families

Andrew Tidmarsh

Grosvenor House
Publishing Limited

This book is published by
Grosvenor House Publishing Ltd
Link House
140 The Broadway, Tolworth, Surrey, KT6 7HT.
www.grosvenorhousepublishing.co.uk

A CIP record for this book
is available from the British Library

ISBN 978-1-83615-355-9

Dedicated to the memory of aunts, uncles, parents and grand-parents who we will never see the likes of again, but were blessed to have known, and the ancestors that bought us to this time and place.

Also to my mother, Doreen Rose Tidmarsh (nee Howard), the last remaining child of Benjamin Howard and Lilian Haymes.

*Dodger*

"The Howard family would like to thank Andrew for his diligence and the hard work he has put in to producing this fantastic publication; we know our father, Ben, would be immensely proud".

Keith, Corinne and Michael Howard – May 2025

# Contents

# Preface

My uncle Ben, Mum's elder brother, kept meticulous records of his family history which I have used extensively along with the kind help of my immediate cousins and the help of my cousin, once removed, Paul Dyer (the grandson of my grandfather's brother Tom), whose enthusiasm and family knowledge was invaluable.

I also thought it important to include the family history of Lilian Haymes, my maternal grandmother, one of the loveliest people I have ever known, who never let her pain and discomfort stop her smile and who was devoted to my grandfather, the man she called 'Dodger.'

This book covers a little history of the Howards and Haymes, two families with their own stories that were joined together when Benjamin met Lilian, a result of events that follow the path of English history to arrive at an ordinary little council house in south London from as far away as Somerset, Hampshire, Warwickshire, Essex and Yorkshire.

I have borrowed heavily from the 'grandparents' book that my uncle kept, containing a wealth of information about his youth and early life as well as his parents and grandparents and a huge basket full of photos that my Mother has.

# Acknowledgements

I would like to express my appreciation to my cousins Corinne Sibley (nee Howard), Keith Howard and Michael Howard for entrusting me with their father's family documents and their help with information and proof-reading.

I would also like to thank Paul Dyer for sharing his experiences and memories of the Howard and Haymes families, a constant source of information.

As well as the genealogy website 'Ancestry.com' that I use extensively in my research, my travels to track down ancestors involve meeting some of what is a small army of people who quietly maintain the ancestral histories of ordinary people, such as parish clerks, registrars and archivists and the people managing the records and maintaining the environment of cemeteries and graveyards across the country whose tireless patience and understanding make life a little more bearable for both the bereaved and the amateur genealogist.

Finally, to my mother, Doreen Tidmarsh (nee Howard), the last remaining child of Benjamin and Lilian, for keeping so many old photos and for her patience with my endless questions.

**Thanks also to:**

Ancestry.com
House of names.com
British History online
Geo. Payne & Co. Archives
Spitalfields Life
Co-operative Women's Guild
Old Deptford History
Local Histories – Bermondsey
L.B. Lewisham Archives

# Introduction

With the help of a genealogy website, family memories and some research I have pieced together a family line, up to and including my Mother, of eleven generations of the Howard family and eight generations of the Haymes family, going back to the early seventeenth century.

At one point, I had stopped at six generations of the Howards from Essex but, after some more digging, found another five generations, three of which originated in Norfolk. I have included those families in Chapter 1 and each chapter thereafter deals with a new generation, with a single chapter dedicated to a short history of the Haymes family.

Family research involves hours of trawling through genealogy websites and old documents, chatting to people whose memories of those days are fast fading and hours of heading in the wrong direction or reaching dead ends. I spent many hours when researching the Tidmarsh's in small parish church offices looking for clues in books that had recorded village baptisms, marriages and deaths for two hundred years.

Writing family histories also allows one the pure pleasure of wandering around graveyards searching for headstones. There are Howard and Haymes graves in Yorkshire, Warwickshire, Devon, Norfolk, Essex, Somerset, Kent and London, that's just the ones I know about. They're not aways marked, however, as many of my ancestors are in common graves in churchyards around the country which could contain up to twenty bodies, so tracking them can be difficult – not impossible, but difficult. Often old gravestones are covered in moss and lichen and impossible to read, but sometimes they're protected by a covering of ivy, which can be peeled away and the residue cleared with a brush. For me, finding a gravestone of one of my ancestors is a real thrill, there's a feeling of connection to a past that I can only imagine, populated with people I never got to meet and will never see the like of again and absolutely worth the effort of scrambling through overgrown churchyards.

I also enjoy looking through old photographs of a black and white world in simpler, harder times with people living their lives who are long gone but who loved and were loved and will never be that young and excited again.

I think it is important that the generations that preceded us are not forgotten by the generations that follow, how else can we understand how we got where we are and where we are going?

So, for all the Howard and Ruberry related families that may read this, whether in the UK, Australia, or anywhere else you choose to roam, this is your story, the story of the two families that made it possible for us to do what we do, where we do it.

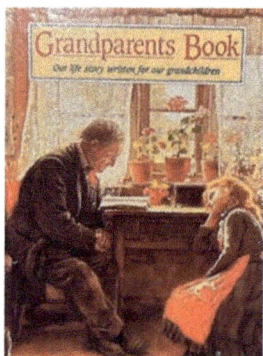

*A Grandparents book, a wonderful idea for capturing memories*

There are many descendants of the Howards and Haymes, most of course, will carry the Howard surname but there are Tidmarsh's, Sibley's, Ruberry's, Trinidad's, Hobb's, Neeling's, Bell's, Matthew's and probably more in the UK and Australia that can trace their ancestry back through the family trees in this book.

I can only hope it creates as much interest in your family history as the reader as it does to me as the writer.

Andrew Tidmarsh February 2025

# Chapter 1:
# History of the Howard name

Sola virtus invicta

Howard

*Howard coat of arms – Virtue alone invincible*

The surname Howard is an ancient name whose history on English soil dates to before the wave of emigration that followed the Norman Conquest of England in 1066. Howard or Howart, is a cognate of the Old Norse name Haward and means "high" or "chief" warden. Occasionally, the surname Howard may have been applied to someone who worked at a dairy farm at which female sheep were kept. In this case, the derivation is from the Old English words "eowu," which means "ewe," and "hierde," which means "herd." The name also came to Britain with the Normans, where it came from the Old French name Huard or the Old German name Howard. The former name is derived from the Old German name Hugihard, which means "heart brave." In other cases, the name was adopted from where the person was born as in "William, son of Roger Fitz Valevine, took the name of Howard from being born in the Castle of Howard, in Wales, in the time of Henry I."

Historical records place Howard amongst the names in use in England at the time of the Conquest. This name has had more than one origin; analysis of surviving ancient records has revealed the Howard family to be descended from Anglo-Saxon tribesmen. Historians have studied documents such as the Domesday Book, and evidence suggests that the name Howard was first found in Norfolk, where one of the first records of the family was Elwin le Heyvard, who was listed in the Hundredorum Rolls of 1273.

The same rolls listed Alice le Heyward in Huntingdonshire and Geoffrey le Hayward in Cambridgeshire. Later, William Heyward or Howard was Sheriff of Norwich, Norfolk in 1657.

"The church of East Winch in Norfolk is a handsome structure in the later English style, with a square embattled tower; in the east window are the arms of Vere and Howard, and on the north side is the ancient chapel of St. Mary, the burial-place of the latter family." Near Grancourt House, which was the seat of Sir William Howard.

Epworth in Lincolnshire was another ancient family seat. "This place, which is the principal town in the Isle of Axholme, a district comprising the north-west portion of the county, was anciently the residence of the Howard family, who had a castellated mansion here, of which nothing now remains except the site, where within the last 70 years have been dug up some of the cannon belonging to the fortifications."

In Westmorland, at Levens in the parish, union, and ward of Kendal another early branch of the family was found. "On the eastern bank of the river Kent, which is crossed by a bridge on the Kendal Road, is Levens Hall, the venerable mansion of the Howards, embosomed in a fine park, and crowned with towers, which, overtopping the highest trees, command extensive prospects on every side. The Howard family built the chapel, a parsonage, and schools, and endowed the living."

Spelling Variations over time: the Howard surname was sometimes spelled Howard and Howerd and these spelling changes often occurred in records referring to the same person, until the Rose Act in 1812, scribes would focus on the sound of a name rather than its spelling.

I selected one of many notable Howards – Thomas Howard (fl. 1698-1703) was a pirate primarily active in the Indian Ocean and the Red Sea during the Golden Age of Piracy!

# Chapter 2:
## History of the Haymes name

The Ancient Arms of

Haymes

The name of Haymes is of Anglo-Saxon origin, the first recorded use of this name was in Cumberland, where the name derives from 'Hames Hall.' Whilst the history of surnames fades into history, those of Anglo-Saxon origin are embedded in a culture that had a lasting impact on English culture. Therefore, descendants of the original Anglo-Saxons have witnessed, have followed, and have been influenced by the history of the English nation.

The Domesday book tells us that our ancestors were originally based in Cumberland, long before the arrival of William in 1066. As with most surnames with English heritage, spellings can vary, until

4

recently when accurate records of birth, death and marriage were mandated as part of the Rose Act in 1812 scribes concentrated on the sound of a person's name rather than the spelling. When originally looking into the Haymes family as part of my book about the Tidmarsh family I assumed my grandmothers name was Haynes, rather than Haymes, which is a more unusual name.

After William's invasion, Anglo-Saxon landowners lost most of their wealth and possessions and fled northward where Norman influence was less pervasive, hence our ancestor's arrival in Cumberland. As the country settled down and peace was restored, the Haymes were recorded as residing in Hames Hall in Papcastle, with a manor and estates to their name. They gradually migrated south to Norfolk, Dorset, and Oxfordshire, where they intermarried with the Hayter family with family seats at The Great Glen and Chadford.

*Hames hall, what the ancestral home of the Haymes family would have looked like in Anglo-Saxon times and the current building*

# Chapter 3:
# 1604 – 1777 – The Norfolk Howards
## From Norfolk to Essex

The Howard family history starts to expand as they relocated to Essex and then south London, but there were three generations of Howard family in Norfolk long before the move southwards.

For the sake of this book, the Norfolk story starts in 1604 in the Norfolk village of Brundall. *(Fig.1)* As we will see further into the book, the parish church plays a central role in village life and assists the amateur genealogist a great deal by being the place where families are baptised, married and buried. They are also one of the few institutions that had clerks and scribes that could read and write, which helps.

John Howard, my great x 9 Grandfather, was born in 1604 in the Norfolk village of Brundall and married Susan Becke from Lynn (King's Lynn) *(see Map 1)*. They had three children quite late in life, Samuel, Anne and in 1646, John. Born when John senior was forty-two and Susan was forty, he was my great x 8 Grandfather, referred to in some records as John Howard II, which I like the sound of.

John 'senior' would have been baptised at St Lawrence parish church in the village *(Fig.2)* but followed tradition and was married in King's Lynn, most likely at the splendid Minster there *(Fig.3)*. It seems like they stayed in the area as their son, John Howard II, was born there. John 'senior's' date of death is unknown, Susan died in 1677 at the age of seventy-one and was buried in Norwich. *(see map 1)*

John Howard II married Hannah Darroch, whose family came from Wingham in Somerset, where she was born in 1648. At the time of meeting John II, her family had moved to King's Lynn and they were married at The Minster, before settling down in the village of Watton *(see Map 1)* Their son Christopher was born there in 1668, baptised at St. Mary's church *(Fig.3)*. Sometime after the birth of their son they moved to Essex to the village of Little Waltham *(see Map 2)*, a village that features in many future generations of Howards as you will see in following chapters. John died at thirty-nine in Saffron Walden *(see Map 2)* when Christopher

### The Norfolk locations and churches, places of Baptism, Marriage and Burial

Fig.1 St Lawrence, Brundall

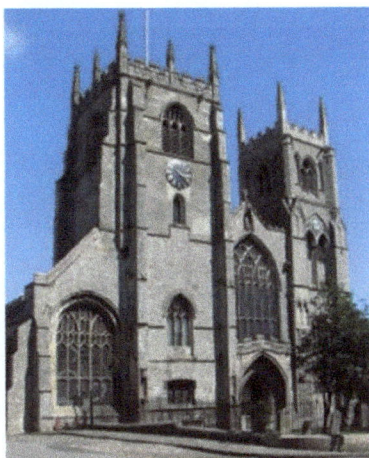

Fig.2 *King's Lynn Minster*

Fig.3 *St Mary's Watton*

*Map 1: C17th Norfolk*

was only seventeen. Hannah eventually returned to her home village of Wingham in Somerset, where she died in 1732 at the age of eighty-four.

Christopher was a favoured name of the Seventeenth-century Howards, much like Benjamin would become in later years.

Christopher, my great x 7 Grandfather, married Hannah Lee, whose family were from Fairseat in Essex. She was born in 1668, and they lived together in Little Waltham all their lives. They had a son, Christopher, who was born in 1697, my great x 6 Grandfather. Hannah died in Little Waltham in 1736 at the age of 68. Christopher 'senior' died in 1730 at the age of sixty-two.

Christopher junior, (who I suppose now becomes senior), married a local girl, Elizabeth Pitts, and they had a son, Christopher (funnily enough) who was born in 1728, my great x 5 Grandfather.

Christopher also married a local girl, Sarah Bentley. Sarah was born in 1730, two years younger than Christopher. Their daughter Sarah was born in 1774 and two years later in 1776, their son William, who's life I will cover in the next chapter was born. Christopher was forty-eight years old, and Sarah was forty-six at that time, so the children were born quite late in their lives. Christopher died at the age of seventy-one in 1799, however, Sarah died in 1777 when William was only one year old, possibly because of complications from the birth.

From the village of Little Waltham, we will continue to the next chapter where the Norfolk Howards establish themselves in Essex before their next move.

# The Norfolk – Essex Family ancestors

## Early Howards C17th - C18th

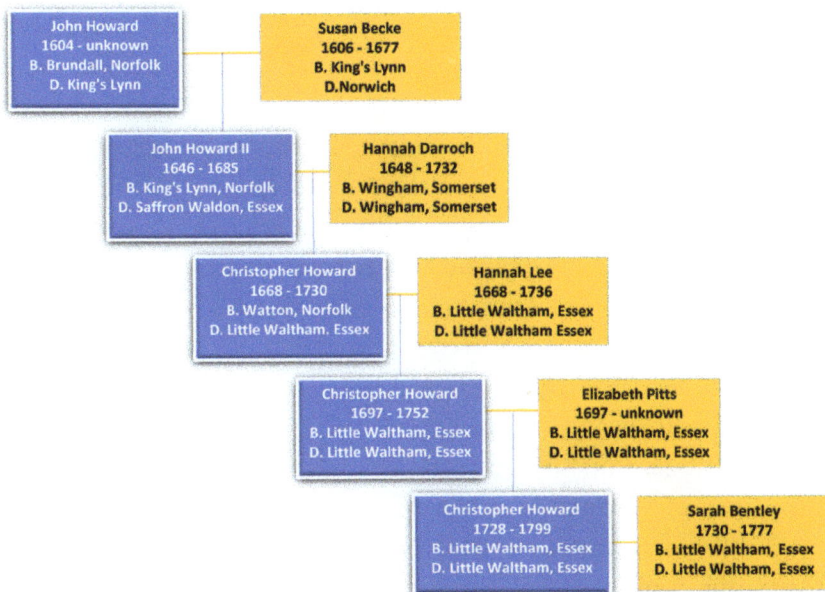

John Howard
1604 - unknown
B. Brundall, Norfolk
D. King's Lynn

Susan Becke
1606 - 1677
B. King's Lynn
D. Norwich

John Howard II
1646 - 1685
B. King's Lynn, Norfolk
D. Saffron Waldon, Essex

Hannah Darroch
1648 - 1732
B. Wingham, Somerset
D. Wingham, Somerset

Christopher Howard
1668 - 1730
B. Watton, Norfolk
D. Little Waltham. Essex

Hannah Lee
1668 - 1736
B. Little Waltham, Essex
D. Little Waltham Essex

Christopher Howard
1697 - 1752
B. Little Waltham, Essex
D. Little Waltham, Essex

Elizabeth Pitts
1697 - unknown
B. Little Waltham, Essex
D. Little Waltham, Essex

Christopher Howard
1728 - 1799
B. Little Waltham, Essex
D. Little Waltham, Essex

Sarah Bentley
1730 - 1777
B. Little Waltham, Essex
D. Little Waltham, Essex

# Chapter 4:
# 1776 – 1817 – William Howard and Mary Ann Reader

## From the market towns of Essex

William Howard, my Gt x 4 Grandfather, was born in 1776 in the village of Little Waltham in Essex and baptised in the parish church of St. Martin, in Wheelers Hill West, the same year. His sister Sarah was baptised two years earlier in 1774 and as we now know, his mother had died a short time after his birth, leaving his father with two very young children.

Little Waltham is a parish and scattered village on the River Chelmer, 4 miles North of Chelmsford, adjacent to the village of Great Waltham. The Domesday Book refers to the two villages singularly as Waltham, 'consisting of several manors.' The area has been inhabited for centuries, one way or another, as the site of an Iron Age village was excavated before the upgrading of the main road north between the current villages. The village straddles the River Chelmer and its main street has a number of old houses near the bridge, notably a rare Essex example of a Wealden hall house. (i)

The Parish Church of St. Martin stands to the East of the village, "the walls are of flint and pebble-rubble mixed with free stone, with limestone dressings; the tower has been repaired with red brick; the roofs are tiled" (ii) The parish church would have been at the centre of village life and here the local Howard families would have been married, baptised, and buried.

Parish church of St. Martin, Little Waltham

Little Waltham, Essex

The general picture of an English village or market town in the 18<sup>th</sup> century was one of a settled society with only a limited amount of movement of people in and out of the town. Most people did tend to live and work within a single settlement, only venturing elsewhere in search of work or, in the case of women, marriage. London has always acted as a form of magnet for migrant workers and did so for the Howards, as we shall see.

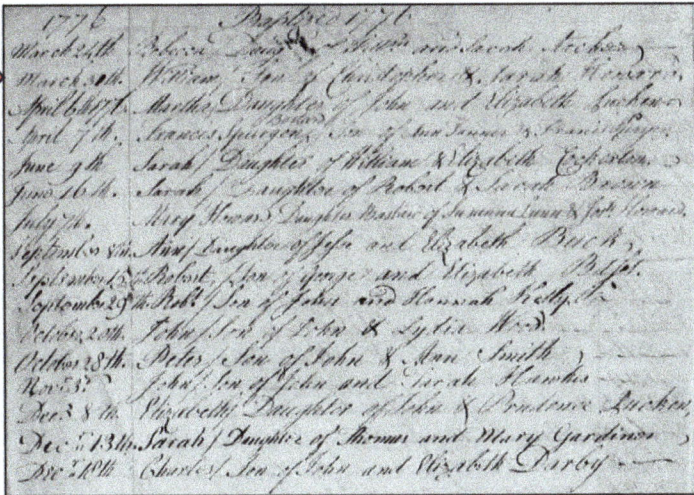

Baptism of William Howard 30<sup>th</sup> March 1776 at St. Martin Church

11

*Late C18th street scene, Little Waltham*

Meanwhile, Jeremiah Reader and his wife Ann Leaven had moved from their home in Linton, Cambridgeshire to the bustling market town of Saffron Walden in Essex, with their children, Mary Ann, born in 1792 and her younger brother William. Like most villages during the eighteenth and nineteenth centuries, life revolved around the parish church and in this respect, the village was gifted with one of the most notable and striking parish churches in Essex, St. Mary the Virgin.

*St. Mary the Virgin*

*Saffron Walden*

William and Mary Ann met and courted, leading up to their marriage on 28<sup>th</sup> March 1815 in Mary Ann's family parish church of St. Mary the Virgin. *(Fig.1)*

After the wedding they moved to the Essex village of Little Ilford *(Fig.2)*, where, after 2 years, Mary Ann gave birth to a son, my great x 3 grandfather, James.

Little Ilford, now part of the London Borough of Newham, was entirely rural at the start of the nineteenth century when the Howards moved there. In 1801, there were just fifteen houses, and the only substantial building was the Three Rabbits pub, an old coaching inn

*Fig. 1 The less grand but, I think, equally attractive parish church of St. Mary the Virgin and Fig.2, Little Ilford, a small unassuming village where the Howards lived for a while, now swallowed up by the expanse of Greater London*

13

that dates to 1630. With a population of around one hundred, it was entirely agricultural, its main crop being osier, a willow like reed used for basket making. However, the population doubled within a decade due to its new claim to fame – a new state of the art jail.

Saffron Walden

Little Waltham

Little Ilford

*Map 2: 18th Century Essex*

## Notes:

(i)     *Source: British history online. A Wealden hall house is a type of vernacular medieval timber-framed hall house traditional in the south east of England. Typically built for a yeoman (land owner), it is most common in Kent (hence "Wealden" for the once densely forested Weald) where there is the highest number surviving buildings and the east of Sussex but has also been built elsewhere.*

(ii)    *Source: British history online*

(iii)   *Source: Comings and goings in 18th Century Saffron Walden ©Hilary Walker*

(iv)    *The neighbouring village of Chesterton was recorded as Cestraforda in 1086. Source: Wikipedia*

14

# Chapter 5:
## 1817 ~ 1878 ~ James Howard and Elizabeth Dunckley
### from Essex to Whitechapel

By the time my great x 3 Grandfather, James, was born, the family had located to Little Ilford in Essex. The census of 1851 has the family home listed as 26 Bakers House, Little Ilford, where the 34-year-old James' profession was recorded as a Chandler, although his marriage certificate in 1838 states his previous profession as Leather Dresser. Thereafter, he is next recorded as being a shopkeeper. Not satisfied with three trades, on the marriage certificate of my great x 2 Grandfather, William James, to Caroline Davis in 1868, his profession is that of a Veterinary Surgeon. A man of many talents.

Meanwhile, in 1809, eight years before the birth of James, in the village of Hordle in Hampshire, Elizabeth Dunckley was born. Elizabeth's father, Joseph, was a cabinetmaker. The family migrated to Whitechapel when Elizabeth was young. James had by now relocated from Little Ilford to Whitechapel, most probably for work as the east London/south Essex areas were becoming more industrialised. By the time James was twenty-one he had met Elizabeth and on 1st April 1838, they were married at St. Mary Magdalene in Bermondsey which at the time was within the county of Surrey. Unfortunately, by the time of the wedding, his father, William, had recently died.

*Marriage certificate, James Howard and Elizabeth Dunckley 1st April 1838,
James was twenty-one, Elizabeth was twenty-nine*

*St. Mary Magdalene parish church, an etching from 1809, the year Elizabeth
was born and a photo taken from the parish website*

Whilst living in Whitechapel, the couple had eight children. Large families were not unusual of course, due to the high mortality rates within the new industrialised areas. I will list their children later and have tried to be as accurate as possible with names and dates, but when researching old records, dates can be random, infant deaths were often followed up with another birth, birth certificates are rare, whereas baptism certificates are more accessible. I tend to use the baptism date as the birth date as often a baptism was conducted very quickly after the birth due to the high risk of the child not surviving. However, if there is a gap between birth and baptism, that can skew your figures somewhat.

16

So, two years into their marriage, the first of eight children arrive, the fourth of which arrived in 1847, my great x 2 Grandfather William James, bringing this chapter to a close and on to the next generation.

*1851 census for James Howard*

Whilst reading the full list of people in James' house, there is also listed Steven Finch, aged fifteen, whose profession was 'servant' originally from Essex and Sophia Wood, aged sixty-four, listed as a 'visitor', originally from Suffolk.

## The children of James and Elizabeth:

| | |
|---|---|
| Mary Ann | born 1839, year of death uncertain. |
| James | born 1840, year of death uncertain. |
| Fanny Emily | born 1842, year of death uncertain. |
| Elizabeth | born 1845, year of death uncertain. |
| **William James** | **born 1847, year of death 1926.** |
| Harriet Maria | born 1849, year of death uncertain. |
| Sophia | born 1850, year of death uncertain. |
| Elizabeth (Eliza) | born 1852, year of death uncertain. |

Other notable events in 1817: George III was monarch, Johann Arfvedson discovered Lithium, the Pentrich rebellion in Derbyshire and James Monroe inaugurated as the 5th President of the United States of America.

I thought it might be relevant at this point to reflect on the area where they lived. Whitechapel was one of the most poor, deprived, and dangerous places in what was to become the greater London area. James and Elizabeth stayed in the Whitechapel area until they died, and their children started their lives here until going their separate ways.

But what was Whitechapel like during the Victorian years of the 19th century?

It was a bustling and diverse neighbourhood located in the East End of London. Known for its extreme poverty levels and overcrowding, the area attracted a mixture of immigrants, including Jews from Eastern Europe and Irish migrants seeking employment in the city. It was notorious for its social issues, as many residents lived in extreme poverty and faced harsh living conditions. The narrow and congested streets were often unsanitary with inadequate housing, and high rates of crime. Epidemics, such as cholera and tuberculosis, were present due to the poor sanitation and overcrowding.

Whilst my great x 2 Grandfather was there, he would have been aware of the series of murders committed by the legendary Jack the Ripper, whose killings occurred in the late 1880s, leaving a lasting impact on the history and portrayal of Whitechapel.

Despite the challenges, like most parts of east London that attracted migrant labourers, Whitechapel thrived within a multicultural atmosphere, being home to a diverse range of cultures and ethnicities, languages, customs, and traditions. This diversity contributed to the rise of industries like tailoring, cabinetmaking and manufacturing. In the later part of the nineteenth century, efforts were made to improve living conditions in the area. Social reformers and philanthropists aimed to address the poverty and overcrowding by establishing institutions, such as schools, hospitals, and charitable organizations. However, these changes often fell short, and it was not until the early twentieth century that significant improvements were seen and by

*Images of Whitechapel during Victorian times that the Howards would have known*

*Whitechapel, 1830's showing the approximate location of Bakers House,
there was a notorious workhouse on Bakers Row, nearby*

then the Howard family had moved away to the coast or south towards Bermondsey and Deptford.

In conclusion, "Whitechapel in the 19th century was an area suffering from poverty, overcrowding, and social challenges. It was a diverse and bustling area, but one that also struggled with unsanitary conditions, crime, and epidemics. Despite its hardships, Whitechapel played a significant role in shaping the social, cultural, and historical fabric of London during this era." (iii)

## The varied occupations of James Howard

Fig.1 1838 at 21 – Leather Dresser

Fig.2 1847 at 30 – shopkeeper

Fig.3 1851 at 34 – Chandler

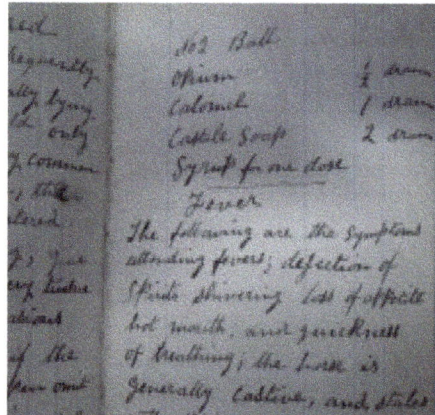

Fig.4 1868 at 51 – Veterinary Surgeon

Fig. 1: Leather-dressing establishments were frequently smaller than tanneries and employed fewer people. It was the task of a currier to dress, finish, and colour tanned hides to make them strong, flexible, and waterproof. There was total interdependency between the tanning and leather-dressing workers.

Fig. 2: Shopkeeper. There are no clues as to the type of shop he either owned or worked at, but he wasn't there for long.

Fig. 3: Chandler, the maker of candles. After the collapse of the Roman empire, trading disruptions made olive oil, the most common fuel for oil lamps, unavailable throughout much of Europe. Therefore, candles became more widely used. Candles were commonplace throughout Europe in the Middle Ages. Candle makers (then known as chandlers) made candles from fats saved from the kitchen

Fig. 4: An excerpt from 'Receipts for Preparing Medicines for Horses and Cattle' circa 1842, including medicinal additives such as opium, calomel, castile soap and gunpowder. Physician James Clark wrote a treatise entitled Prevention of Disease in which he argued for the professionalization of the veterinary trade, and the establishment of veterinary colleges. This was finally achieved in 1790 and the opening of a veterinary college in London. The Royal College of Veterinary Surgeons was established by royal charter in 1844. Veterinary science came of age in the late 19th century.

## Notes:

(i)    Part of the ancient parish of Bermondsey St. Mary was incorporated into a new ecclesiastical parish (an administrative area within the Church of England) until 1956, when it was abolished. Part went to Bermondsey St Mary Magdalene with St Olave and St John and part to St Stephen, Southwark.

(ii)   I have listed the eight children that I have so far accounted for, there could be 2 or 3 others. There are unconfirmed records of an Emily and Maria Jeanette, both born in 1850, with no recorded burial dates that I can find thus far.

(iii)  Source: "19th Century events and developments"

# Chapter 6:
# 1847 – 1926 – William James Howard and Caroline Davis

## from Whitechapel to Deptford and the Coast

From this point, the gathering of family information becomes a little easier and this chapter starts with William James Howard, son of James Howard and Elizabeth Dunckley and my great x 2 Grandfather. Born into the maelstrom that was nineteenth century Whitechapel, the fifth child and second son of a family of eight children.

He was apprenticed, at an early age, to a building company where he trained to be a bricklayer, the occupation he had before becoming a stationer. *(i)* At that time, the family home had moved from Whitechapel to the south London village of Deptford, at 9 Rutford Road, within the parish of St. Paul, referred to at that time as within both the counties of Kent and Surrey, depending on what road you lived in.

Deptford, for those who may not know is an area on the south bank of the River Thames in southeast London. It is named after a ford of the River Ravensbourne. From the mid-sixteenth to the late nineteenth century it was home to Deptford Dockyard, established by Henry VIII, the first of the Royal Dockyards, associated with the knighting of Sir Francis Drake by Queen Elizabeth I aboard the *Golden Hind*, the legend of Sir Walter Raleigh laying down his cape for Elizabeth, Captain James Cook's third voyage aboard HMS *Resolution*, and the mysterious alleged murder of Christopher Marlowe in a house along Deptford Strand.

The result of a conjoining of two communities, one at the ford and one from a nearby fishing village, Deptford's two communities grew together and flourished during the period when the docks were the main administrative centre of the Royal Navy, but declined when the Royal Navy moved out. The commercial docks declined until their closure in 2000, leaving the area a shadow of its former self before being absorbed by the newly created London Borough of Lewisham.

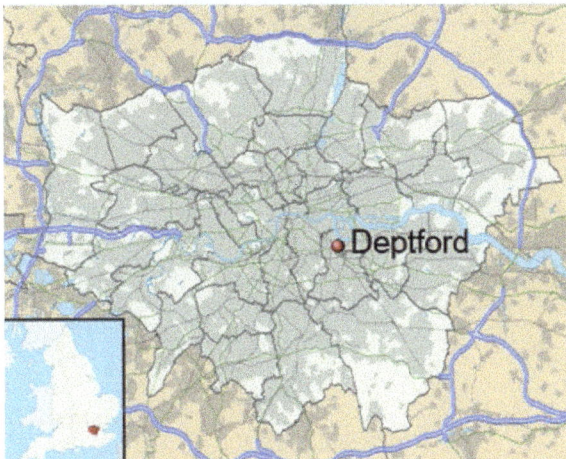

*Present day Deptford, the statue of an anchor acting as a reminder of its glory days as a major dockyard, its history as a union of local communities dependent on the river absorbed into Greater London*

*(i)   The profession of Stationer in Victorian times was often given to a bookseller,
as well as magazines and writing utensils*

*Images from early nineteenth century Deptford, a bustling
Thames-side dockyard community*

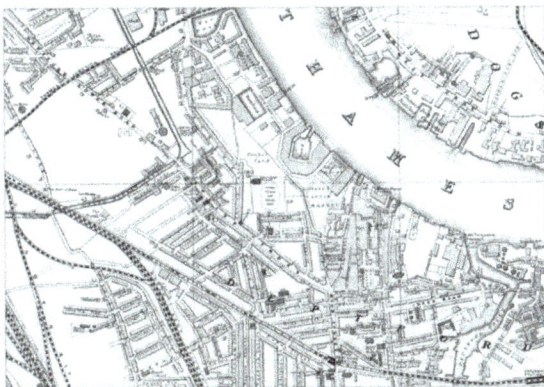

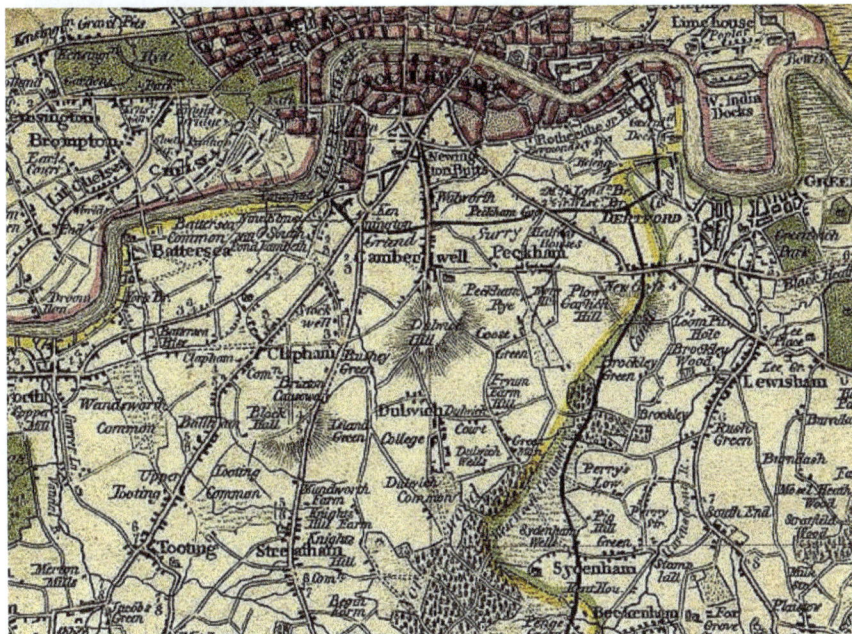

*A beautiful map of south London, drawn up at the time of William and Carolines residence in Deptford, showing the borders of both Kent and Surrey dissecting Deptford village*

For a short while, we'll leave Deptford and travel to Margate on the Kent coast. In its day, the perfect seaside town for the peoples of London and Kent, it may have lost some of its glory as people became more mobile and holidays abroad became popular, but I, like many children of my generation, remember summer days spent there on its seemingly endless beach with all the usual seaside paraphernalia, including donkeys!

The reason for mentioning Margate at this point was the Davis family. Residing at 30 King Street, Samuel Ashby Davis, a mariner, his wife Catherine Baker Davis and their three daughters, Caroline, born in 1847, Elizabeth Hannah, born in 1849, Emily Hannah, born in 1850. Their son, Henry William, was born in 1852, but sadly died at the age of 5 in 1857.

Carolines family can be traced back to the Canterbury area in Kent for at least five generations that I've found so far.

Caroline would become my great x 2 Grandmother and sometime before her 21st birthday she met and was courted by William James. Quite where they met, I do not know but as was often the custom, he travelled from the family home in Whitechapel to Margate to marry in his wife's local church. They were both twenty-one years of age when they married on twenty-seventh of July 1868 at St. Johns parish church, Margate. *(Fig.2)* His marriage certificate has his profession as 'Stationer.' *(Fig.1)*

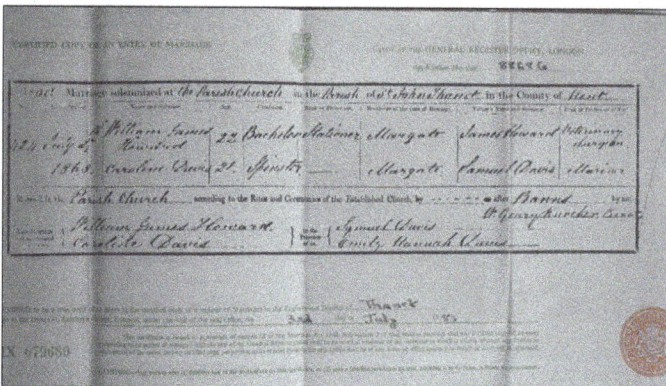

*Fig.1 Marriage certificate of William James to Caroline at the parish church of St. Johns, Margate, 27th July 1868*

*Fig.2 St. Johns parish Church, then and now – which witnessed the baptism of the Davis sisters, the marriage of Caroline's parents, Samuel and Catherine and Caroline's marriage to William*

## Margate, as the Davis family would have known it

*C19th photo of the beach in all its Victorian splendour, coloured*

*King Street, early 1900's home of the Davis family.*

At this point, we leave the sunny shores of Margate and return to the riverside village of Deptford. The couple lived at 37 Edale Road, a drab tree-lined terrace comprising 2/3-bedroom houses in a rundown part of Deptford. William's profession at this point was still Stationer, but he changed professions in his forties, where in the 1891 census he was a general labourer, before ending his days as a lead worker.

*1911 Census, just the two of them in Edale Road, 10 years later Caroline would die in Folkestone, Kent*

From Edale road, the family moved to a new home at 9 Rudford road, where most of their children were born.

William and Caroline were married for fifty-three years and had eleven children that I can verify, there could have been two more, but I'll stick with what I know for sure. At the time of the 1921 census, of their eleven children, only seven had survived. I know that William and John didn't survive to see 1921, but not sure who the other two were. They were both living on their own when Caroline died at the age of seventy-four on the fifth of March 1921 but even though the census recorded her as living in Deptford, she was buried in Folkestone. The service was carried out at the parish church of St. Mary and St Eanswythe, in Church Street. Five years later, in 1926, William died at the age of seventy-nine. The death was registered in the borough of Greenwich, so I will assume he was still based at the family home in Rudford Road. I do not know why Caroline was in Folkestone and not Deptford, or even her hometown of Margate, it is likely the reason will never be known.

28

*The parish church of St. Mary and St Eanswythe, Folkestone*

## The children of William James and Caroline Howard:

| | |
|---|---|
| Emily Catherine | born 1869, died 1946 – married to Joseph Markham (1869 – 1946) |
| William Henry | born 1870, died 1915 – married Loisa (Letty) Langridge (1875 – 1960) |
| Catherine Elizabeth | born 1873, date of death unknown. |
| **Benjamin Harwood** | **born 1883, died 1964 – my great Grandfather.** |
| Henry Alfred | born 1874, date of death unknown. |
| Joseph Dunkley | born 1878, died 1936, named after his grandmother |
| Samuel Davis | born 1879, died 1960, named after his mother's family, buried in Nunhead cemetery. |
| George Edward | born 1880, date of death unknown. |
| Thomas Robine | born 1884, date of death unknown. |
| John Wheeler | born 1888, died 1889. |

Other notable events in 1847: Victoria was monarch, a general election in UK resulted in the Whigs in control and the worst year of the Irish famine.

# Chapter 7:
# 1883 – 1964 – Benjamin Harwood and Sarah Ann (Frances)
## from Deptford to Bermondsey

When researching family history, I use a website called Ancestry. com, for which I have a subscription, you can set up as many family trees as you like – I have 4 currently – but the cool thing is, it lets you know who is also researching your ancestors and as long as they have given permission to be contacted, you can send them a message. Whilst researching my great Grandfather, Benjamin Harwood, I noticed he was part of a family tree being written by someone else. So, I contacted them and got a response from the guy who was putting the tree together, turns out we were related. Paul Dyer was the grandson of my great Uncle Tom, so we shared the same great grandparents. We met several times to find graves around London and his family knowledge is excellent, but more of our grave hunting later.

This chapter dwells on some interesting characters. I find that when writing about family history, I gravitate to certain people and Sarah Ann is one of them.

But first, to recap, Benjamin Harwood Howard was born in 1883, the fourth child and second son of William James and Caroline.

As a child, the family home was at 9 Rudford Road, Deptford, shared with ten siblings, so the house would have been cosy.

*A snapshot of the family in Rudford Road from the 1891 census*

Benjamin Harwood seems to have been what I can only describe as a character. It is unlikely he had an education as he could neither read nor write. He would often visit my grandparents on a Sunday afternoon, walking the route from his home in Deptford to their house in Bellingham, very often in a state of inebriation and if not, he would depart soon after arrival for the nearby social club or pub. He had several jobs as a general labourer, but ended his working days as a Boiler Fireman, or Stoker as they are sometimes called, with the Borough Council. In his late teens he met and courted a local girl, Sarah Ann Martin and at the ages of twenty-one, on the twenty-fifth of February 1904 they married in the parish church of St. Olav, (i) in Tooley Street, Bermondsey. *(Fig.1)*

St Olave, Tooley St. 1913.

Edward Yates

Fig.1 St. Olav's church, Bermondsey, then and now

They moved into a house at 218 Lynton Road and within a
year, in 1905, their daughter Catherine was born, followed in 1906
with the birth of their first son, Benjamin, my grandfather and then,
in 1908, a second son, Thomas.

Modern Lynton Road, Bermondsey

The 1911 census, Benjamin, a general labourer at that time and three young children

## Benjamin Harwood and Frances

Benjamin Harwood Howard, looking the epitome of an early C20th working man and a snip from a family photo from the early 1900's of Frances, a dearly loved woman with a wonderful smile. Look at the difference between their expressions for the camera. Note also the three-piece suit with watch fob, starched collar (made by Frances), cloth cap and I suspect, highly polished boots.

*The Howard family, taken from the 1921 census, with Benjamin (my grandfather) already working at George Payne & Co. Tea Merchants*

Benjamin's employment as a Boiler Fireman by Bermondsey Borough Council was recorded by my uncle in his book. He would have worked at the Town Hall, a grand Victorian building *(Fig.2)*, heated by huge boilers in the basement. The building was bombed in WW2 and demolished in 1963. It was never rebuilt, as post-war Bermondsey became part of the London Borough of Southwark and Town Hall business was conducted elsewhere. Benjamin would have been in his sixties during the blitz so, if he was working, he would have gone back to general labouring for the Council works department in Bermondsey.

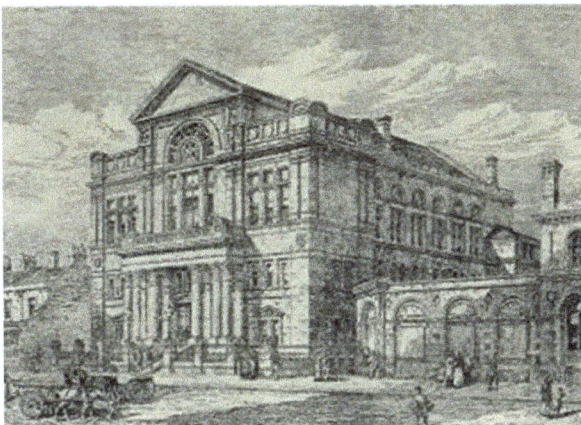

*Fig.2 The magnificent façade of Bermondsey Town Hall before its destruction, where my great Grandfather kept the boilers fed*

35

Opinions about Benjamin Harwood seem to be mixed, he no doubt inherited the stubbornness of the Howards (often reflected in my mother), he was often inebriated and memories of him seem to be sparse and a little cloudy. The same cannot be said of my great Grandmother, whose given name was Sarah Ann but preferred to be called Frances, so that, from now on, is how I will refer to her.

A brief overview of Frances' family:

She was a member of the Martin family from Kent who lived in villages around Tunbridge Wells.

Her great Grandfather was Thomas Martin (1771 – 1850) from Brenchley and her great Grandmother was Frances Piper, (1775 – 1855) from Ticehurst in Sussex.

Her grandfather was Alfred Martin (1819 – 1878) from Brenchley and her grandmother was Mary Reed (1812 – 1886) from Lamberhurst in Kent.

Her father was George Martin (1847 – 1905) a labourer and her mother was Mary Ann Drummond (1847 – 1929), both from Tudely, Kent.

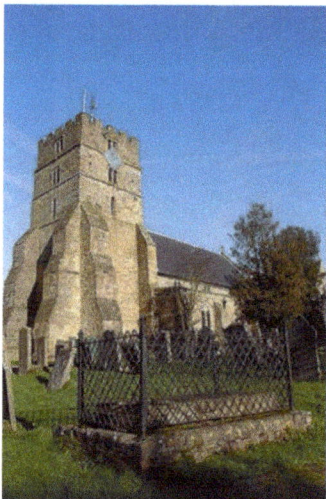

*All Saints parish church, Brenchley*

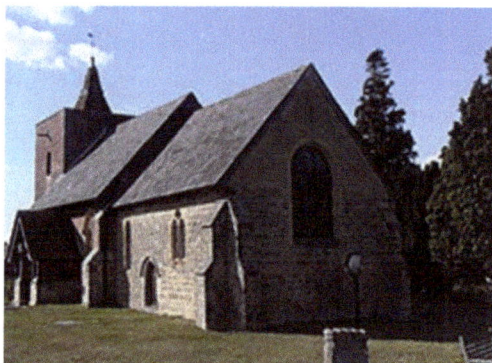

*All Saints parish church, Tudely*

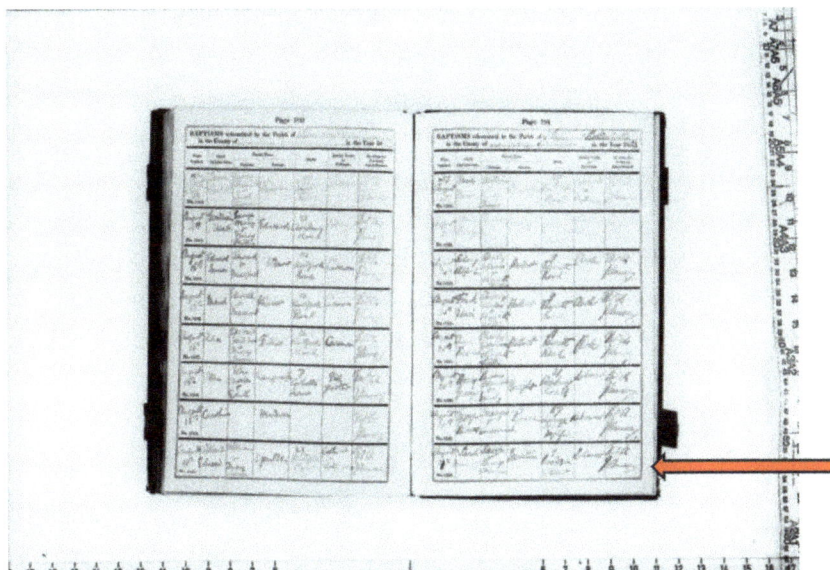

*Birth certificate of Frances Martin*

By 1883, the Martin family had resettled in Bermondsey at 9 Godson Road, Frances was baptised on twenty-first of August 1883 at St. Barnabus church in Rotherhithe.

*Parish church of St. Barnabus, Rotherhithe*

*Traffic jam, Bermondsey, 1906*

37

Within four years, they were a family of five and had relocated to nearby Lynton Road. Benjamin was a general labourer until his job at the Town Hall and Frances made white stiff collars at home.

For the benefit of any younger readers, you will see from the earlier photos that men's shirts were often collarless (hence the modern term 'grandad shirt'), so that that the shirt could be worn casually and to make it more formal, a separate collar could be added, which would have been made of a highly starched fabric, attached with a stud, as modelled by Benjamin below. *(Fig.3)*

*Fig.3 Starched shirt collars and studs*

## The children of Benjamin Harwood and Frances:

**Catherine** – affectionately known as Kate, born on 24th November 1904. She married Alfred Howes on the 25th of December 1928 in a civil registration ceremony held at St. Barnabus parish church Plough Way, Rotherhithe, London. They lived at 18 Strathnairn Street, Bermondsey, where Alfred worked as a Wharf Landing Clerk. He was born in 1900 and died in 1971. They had one daughter, Eileen who was born in 1930.

Catherine died on the third of July 1985; they are buried together in Camberwell New Cemetery.

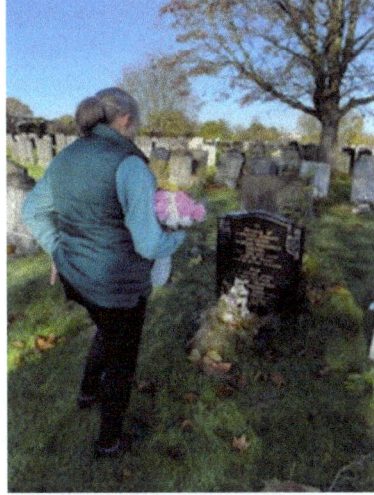

*Life is full of small coincidences; here is the grave of Catherine and Alfred in the same cemetery as Karen's maternal grandparents.*

Their daughter, Eileen married Antonio Alfonso Menditta (1929 – 2007) in 1964. Eileen died recently in 2022, they both lived and were buried in Liskeard, Cornwall.

I don't know much about Catherine, I know that my grandfather, Benjamin, was very fond of her but anecdotes are sparse.

**Thomas –** Thomas Stephen Howard was born in October 1908 and was baptised on the seventeenth of January 1909 at St. Mary Magdalene church, Bermondsey. He married Rose Lilian Kirk in a civil registration ceremony on the second of June 1931 at St. Barnabus church, Rotherhithe, London. Thomas and Rose lived at 218 Lynton Road, Bermondsey and had three children, Joan Iris in 1932 and in 1946, twins Maureen and Anthony.

Joan married Arthur Thomas Dyer (1931 – 2017). Their son, Paul is the cousin I went grave hunting with on several occasions. At the time of writing, Joan is still alive and living in Bermondsey.

Maureen married Victor Hussey in a civil registration ceremony in July 1970 and died recently in 2023. Victor Hussey is still alive.

Anthony, Maureen's twin married Pauline Clarke and to my knowledge, at time of writing, they are both alive.

Fair to say that Thomas and Rose were very popular, with both friends and family. My mother remembers him as tall, handsome, and always very well dressed.

*Tom and Rose*

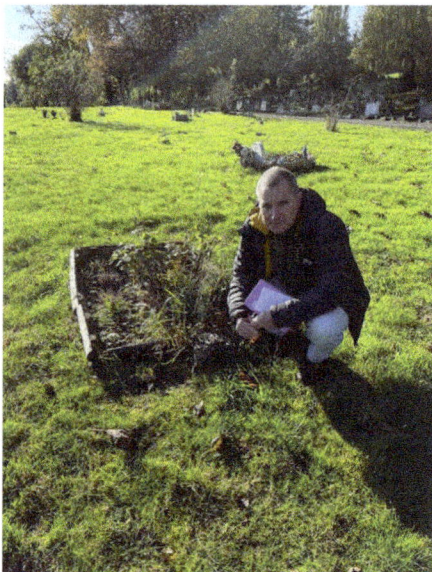

*At the unmarked grave of my great Uncle, Thomas Stephen Howard*

Thomas' occupation was 'Manager and Buyer for hospitals and institutions,' he was the first person in his street to own a motor car, which was virtually unheard of at the time. He was also the first person in his street to own a television set. He bought it so that he could invite people round to watch the coronation in 1953. Unfortunately, they could not get the set to work, so everyone deported to the pub to watch it there!

In the early days of WW2 when children were being evacuated out of London, my mother, Doreen, was sent to live with a family in the village of Menheniot, in Cornwall. She was evacuated with her sister, Sheila. However, Sheila struggled with being away from home and cried constantly. It was clear that she would have to be collected, and it was my great Aunt Rose who accompanied her sister-in-law Lilian to Cornwall to collect her and take her back to the family home in Bellingham. This left my mother on her own for quite a while until she could come back, which she was very unimpressed about. My mother was seven at the time, when she told me this story, she was ninety-two and she was still moaning about it.

Last year, whilst on a short holiday in Cornwall, I visited Menheniot. The people there were very kind to the children evacuated there, and my mother has fond memories of the place (apart from being left on her own, obviously). It was quite strange wandering around a small village where my mother would have had to make a life for herself away from everything and everyone that she knew. It's as though you can hear ghosts from the past in the noises from the nursery school in the old schoolhouse and the silence from the church that stands like a sentinel on the top of the hill in the middle of the village, silently watching the centuries plod by.

Thomas died in October 1966 aged just 57 and was buried at Camberwell New Cemetery in a plot with no headstone, positioned on a hill within the cemetery which was quite difficult to find at first as there were hardly any other graves around, so it was hard to work out the plot number. But eventually, I found it.

So, back to Benjamin Harwood. Having no education, he would have found his choice of occupations limited and general labouring was always a good fallback to make a living. Labouring was a hard, brutal existence, not least when he started as a stoker for the borough council. Back breaking work, but it was indoors, warm, and close to home. Always good to look on the bright side I suppose.

I cannot say whether the image of labourers below represented the work that Benjamin undertook, neither do I know how, if at all, the General Strike (ii) affected him.

*A nice image I found of early C20th labourers*

*Benjamin would have been 43 at the time of the 1926 General Strike*

*Hot, back-breaking work, the life of a boiler fireman*

After the death of his wife Frances on the eleventh of December 1930 he went to live with Tom and Rose at Lynton Road and that is where he stayed for 34 years until his death at the age of 81 in October 1964.

Benjamin Harwood Howard was put to rest in an unmarked common grave (iii) at Camberwell New Cemetery. I sourced the plot number from 'find my grave' but after an unsuccessful visit, failed to find it, fortunately, I revisited with Paul Dyer, and he showed me where it was. It is the most unassuming grave, hard to find without spending time searching amongst the undergrowth in a long-forgotten part of the old cemetery.

Other notable events in 1883: Victoria was monarch and had reigned for 54 years, the eruption of Krakatoa, the opening of the Brooklyn Bridge and the assassination of US president James Garfield.

*The last resting place of Benjamin Harwood Howard, a common grave situated in between the two headstones in the foreground*

Frances Howard was fondly remembered and sadly missed, she died at the age of forty-seven on the eleventh of December 1930, my Mum was not born, and her sister Sheila was born two months after she died. My uncle Ben remembers her, she used to empty her tea caddy for him so he could play with it.

Frances was a devout Roman Catholic and always wore a rosary around her neck, tucked into the inside of her dress. When I told mum about this, she thought she had one somewhere, which I found strange as she was never particularly religious, but when she found it, we realised that it belonged to Frances. When Frances became ill, she was taken to the Rotherhithe and Bermondsey Infirmary in Deptford Lower Road (now Lower Road), which would become St. Olavs Hospital, before its extensive damage in bombing raids, which led to its eventual absorption into newer hospitals. *(Fig.1)*

Rotherhithe & Bermondsey Infirmary.

*Fig.1 Rotherhithe & Bermondsey infirmary was opposite St. Olave's Poor Law Union Workhouse and was built because of the requirements of the Metropolitan Poor Act of 1867, which required that infirmary accommodation be separate from workhouse buildings*

On her death, she was taken back to Lynton Road and placed in the front room in an open coffin, as was often the custom, so that people could pay their last respects. There is a story that candles were set up in the room around the coffin. When the house was empty, Benjamin blew them all out because he thought they were dangerous.

Frances was buried in St. Patricks Roman Catholic cemetery in Leytonstone, east London. She was taken by horse and carriage, however, on its arrival, there was a problem. It was customary at the time, possibly still is, that for a Roman Catholic funeral, the horses should be all black. One of the horses that arrived had a white patch on one of its legs. There then followed a mild panic whilst a solution was sought. The solution arrived in the form of some coal dust collected from the house, which was used to hide the white patch and so, the funeral could continue.

I visited St. Patricks cemetery early in 2024 with Paul Dyer. A lovely, peaceful oasis in the middle of this busy east London suburb and a quite spectacular place. The same family have been looking after this cemetery for three generations and the latest manager, the daughter and granddaughter of the last two managers gave us a guided tour.

Frances lays in an unmarked common grave, in a quiet corner of the cemetery. On the day I was there it was eerily quiet, and I felt a feeling of elation on finding her resting place, but regret that we never got a chance to meet.

*Benjamin Harwood and Frances, taken in the garden of Lynton Road*
*(courtesy of Paul Dyer)*

# Burial Documentation

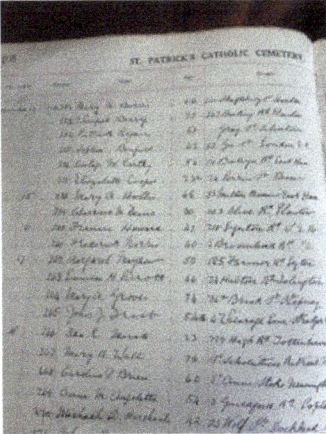

Burial Register, in the name
of Frances

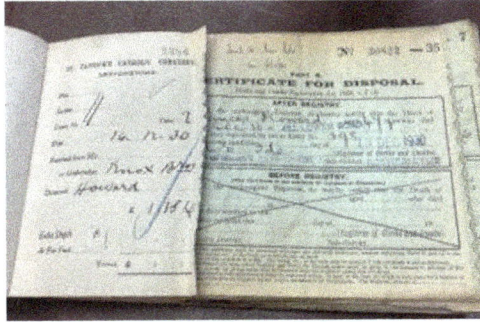

Certificate of disposal

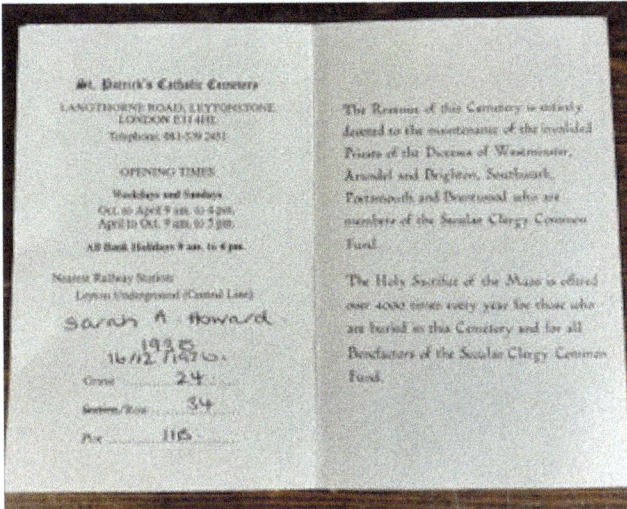

plot location

*The last resting place of Frances Martin*

*An unmarked grave tucked away in a quiet corner of St. Patrick's Cemetery: "Leytonstone's most atmospheric corner." Home to 170,000 graves, including the Hitchcock family and Jack the Ripper's last victim, managed by the same family for 3 generations*

*One of the few photos I could find of Frances. From L-R: Back – My Uncle Benjamin, great uncle Tom, my grandfather, Benjamin. Front – Mrs Horwood, wife of George Alfred Horwood (iv), mayor of Bermondsey, my grandmother, Lilian, my great Grandmother Frances*

*A young Frances with (L-R) Benjamin, Catherine & Thomas. I don't know whose baby she is holding*

# Notes:

(i)    The name St. Olav crops up several times when researching people and places in Bermondsey. In early C20th, Southwark St Olave was an ancient civil and ecclesiastical parish on the south bank of the River Thames, covering the area around where Shard London Bridge now stands in the modern London Borough of Southwark, ultimately named after St. King Olaf II of Norway. The boundaries varied over time, but in general the parish stretched east from London Bridge past Tower Bridge to St Saviour's Dock

(ii)   The general strike of 1926 lasted nine days, from 4 to 12 May. It was called by the General Council of the Trades Union Congress (TUC) in an unsuccessful attempt to force the British government to act to prevent wage reductions and worsening conditions for 1.2 million locked-out coal miners. Some 1.7 million workers went out, especially in transport and heavy industry.

(iii)  A common grave is a grave that belongs to the cemetery owner. Unlike a private grave that is purchased by a family or individual, a common grave serves a commercial purpose. They could often contain 10-12 bodies over time.

(iv)   I am not sure what the event was here, but it seems like quite a jolly occasion, The son of the Horwood's, Alec George, was awarded a VC in WW2

# Chapter 8:
## 1906 – 2006 – Benjamin and Lilian
### 'Dodger' and 'Sissy', from Bermondsey to Bellingham

My grandfather, Benjamin Howard, was born on Thursday the fifth of July 1906 at St. Olav's hospital in Bermondsey, the second child and eldest son of Benjamin Harwood Howard and his wife, Frances Martin. Edward VII was on the throne; San Fransico was almost destroyed by an earthquake and William Kellogg invented cornflakes. A wonderful caring, funny man who always had a 'mop of curly hair' always very well dressed as a younger man.

*Benjamin Howard*

Quick-witted, intelligent and with a gift for processing numbers, always well dressed (in his earlier days anyway) and with a mop of curly hair, often to be seen in a bowler hat, he lived in the family home in Lynton Road until he was married.

He attended Monnow Road school, Bermondsey and was a gifted and well-liked student who qualified for a scholarship at Christ College, a prestigious school in North Finchley. He had to decline the offer as the family could not afford to send him there. So, at 14, he was forced to go to work, but how different his life may have been.

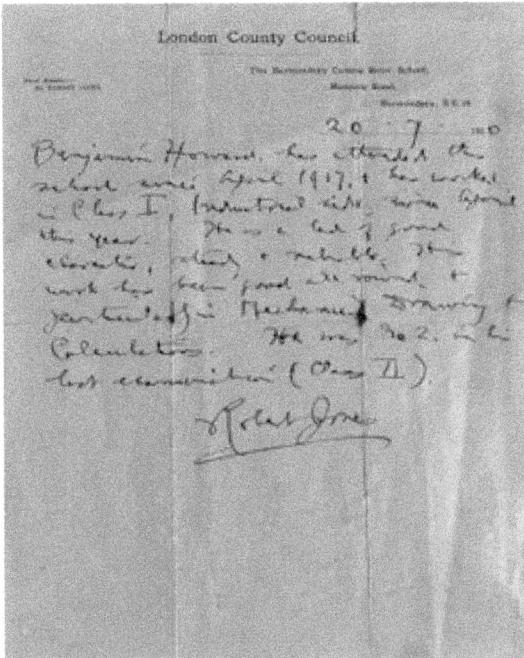

*School report from 1920, when Benjamin was 14, what was to be his last year of school before starting work. "Benjamin Howard has attended this school since April 1917 and has worked in class1, industrial side, since April this year. He is a lad of good character, steady and reliable. His work has been good all round, particularly in mechanical drawing and calculations. He was no.2 in last examination" Robert Jones*

*The imposing façade of Christ College, Finchley, where Benjamin was granted a scholarship but was unable to attend due to the cost*

At 14 he went to work as a tea boy at George Payne & Co, a Tea & Coffee Merchant. They were based in a factory in Queen Elizabeth Street, near Tower Bridge Road, London SE1. The company was primarily involved in blending and packing tea for Brooke Bond and Sainsbury's own-brand products but also diverged into other beverages and confectionary – some of us will remember Paynes 'poppets,' which was them. They are still in business but are part of the Northern Foods conglomerate. He was a 'tea boy' with a difference. His job was to boil water and prepare teas for tasting. If they weren't correct, he had to make another dozen cups. He was particularly proud of the fact that Mr. Alfred Sainsbury when buying his teas, regularly came over to have a chat with him as he himself served an apprenticeship at George Payne until joining the family business in 1906.

*Sainsbury's teas, tasting prepared by Ben Howard*

*Alfred Sainsbury*

After four years, he left George Payne to work as an office clerk for a Potato and Pea merchant at Spitalfields, London's largest fruit and vegetable market. His experience as an office boy with a good head for figures made him an excellent candidate for a small market business. His writing was beautiful, he was meticulous in his work, and he had the ability to manage two sets of books, a valuable skill in some companies at the time.

*Spitalfields market in its prime, showing one of the merchants that traded there.*
*This photo was taken in 1928, when Benjamin was 22, working in the*
*offices of E. Wakefield*

Whilst working at Spitalfields, in his late teens, he met and courted Lilian Haymes, who would become my maternal grandmother.

Born in 1904, Lilian Elizabeth Haymes was two years older than Benjamin and after their courtship they moved in with Lilian's parents at their new address of 34 Kipling Street, Bermondsey.

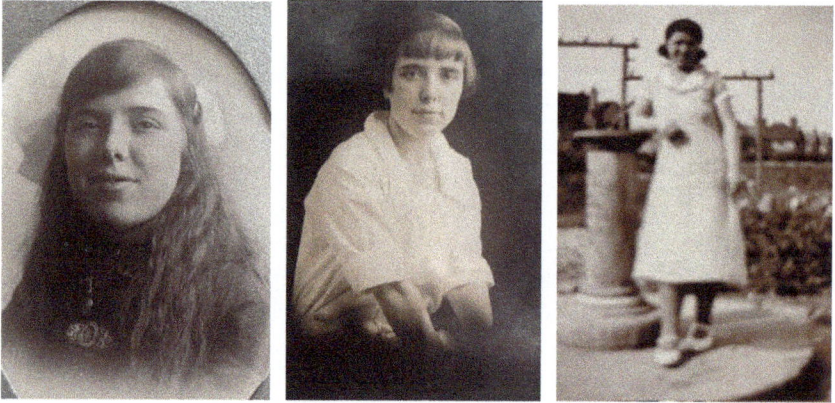

*Lilian Elizabeth Haymes*

They married on the twenty-sixth of December 1926 at St. Annes church, Bermondsey. Lilian was six months pregnant at the time and their first child, Benjamin, was born on the thirtieth of March 1927.

*St. Annes Church, Bermondsey*

*Marriage certificate*

For the first two years of their marriage, they continued to live with the in-laws in Kipling Street. Just to give a picture of what life was like for working class people, there were four adults and a baby living in a 2-bedroom house, there was no bathroom, the toilet was a small whitewashed building outside in the back yard, toilet paper was cut up telehone directories and baths were taken in a large tin bath in front of an open fire. After two years, Benjamin, Lilian and Benjamin jnr moved to a top floor flat opposite no 34 where they stayed for a short while, my uncle remembers there being bugs in the wallpaper – so in 1931 the family moved to a house in Alderminster Road,Bermondsey.

*Early married life*

*Kipling Street, Bermondsey*

Kipling Street and Alderminster roads were a short walk to Long Lane, which housed one of the first Eel and Pie shops in south London, the original 'fast food' outlets, eat in or take-away, the food, wooden floors, tables and benches fascinated my uncle, as did the smells that filled the air.

*Eel and Pie shops, eat in or takeaway, a real culinary treat and still around today. I could not find a record of a pie & mash shop in Long Lane, but there used to be one, Rootes, located in Tooley street, 10 mins walk away)*

*A lovely photo, taken in 1933 in the doorway of 34 Kipling Street, with Lilian in the background and (L-R) Sheila, Doreen and Benjamin*

Alderminster Road in the mid-nineteen-thirties was typical of city life at that time, with a 'muffin man' selling wares from a tray balanced on his head, ringing a bell to announce his arrival, a 'cats meat' man, with skewers of meat for cats and dogs, horse drawn vans, roads covered in horse manure, which the driver was supposed to clear up (hence the bucket and shovel hanging from the back of most horse drawn vehicles).

Once the house next door caught fire, the owner dropped a half-a-crown coin and looked for it under his sofa, using a match for illumination. I have no idea if he found it.

Most Sundays, Benjamin and his children would walk to East Street market in Walworth, close to The Old Kent Road, they would be treated to a glass of sarsaparilla – a fizzy drink made from the root of the sarsaparilla plant, with a taste like root beer, apparently – and allowed to share a bowl of jellied eels. On the way back, as was customary on a Sunday for many years, Benjamin would buy shellfish from a stall outside the Dun Cow pub in the Old Kent Road which would be eaten at teatime. The dream though was always to move into a proper house that could be the basis for a settled family home and very soon all his hard work was to pay off.

The family spent four years at Alderminster Road until moving to a new house at 23 Grangemill Road, Bellingham, London SE6 a semi-detached three bedroom house on a sweeping council estate, on the edge of Catford. It had decent size bedrooms, a coal cellar, a large kitchen, a bathroom, a downstairs toilet and much to my grandfathers delight, a front and back garden. *(see Appendix 1)*

My grandfather was a prolific gardener, an expert in using every square inch of soil to its best effect. The garden was divided into two sections with a small path in the middle and a tiny patch of grass in one corner that my grandmother had to negotiate extremely hard to keep. The front garden was primarily her domain because it contained flowers, and he was strictly a fruit and veg man.

## Bermondsey life, 1930's

*The cat's meat man*

*Horse drawn vans*

*The muffin man*

Although money was sparse, they still managed holidays to Brighton, where they stayed at a boarding house owned by one Mrs Judge and sometimes Great Yarmouth, transported by Timpsons Coaches of Catford, and occasional visits to Lilians parents, Burman and Eliza Haymes.

*Holiday, Yarmouth*

*'be relaxed – travel by coach'*

*Holiday, Brighton*

Benjamin remained working at Spitalfields until his retirement. This involved very early starts. Lilian would get up at 04:00 AM every working day to cook a fried breakfast, see Benjamin off to work and go back to bed. For forty-seven years, I'll just let that sink in. Benjamin would then cycle to work – 8.7 miles, approximate duration 50 minutes – or catch a train to Cannon Street and walk 2 miles to work.

My grandfather was a great fan of fried food, and they became my grandmother's speciality, as my brother Robert will confirm. After Lilian died, my mother used to take him over fruit cake, his favourite, which we would promptly slice – and fry in lard. I can't say I've ever tried it but never say never.

During WW2, Benjamin was a fire warden, fully kitted out with an armband and tin helmet. Outside of the house was a stirrup pump and hose as well as buckets of sand and water for putting out small fires caused by bombing raids. At the end of the War, he cut the brass nozzle off the hose and attached it to his garden hose. However, in 1995, after a mere fifty-six years, the leather washer seized up and he complained that he couldn't find a replacement.

*The offending hose nozzle, still in possession of my cousin, still the property of HMG*

Maybe now is the time to explain why his nickname was Dodger, it was because he always had a 'dodge', usually to save money (remember the fire warden hose nozzle). He would make his own tools (I have some in my shed, they are substantial!), he would wander around the estate and pick up old wood or anything else that he thought he could use in the garden and would generally recycle anything that could be reused, he hated waste. When he was younger, he told me that there were a group of neighbours who kept geese for slaughter at Christmas. One person would house them, one would provide food, one would provide bedding, on a rotational basis so that it was a co-operative effort.

Lilian also had a nickname of 'Sissy' it started with her siblings but also caught on with her sister-in-law Lou, wife of her brother Maurice, who continued to call her that until the end.

Benjamin was too young to enlist in WW1, he was only eight, and too old to enlist for WW2 as he was thirty-three years old, but he served in the Royal Army Pay Corps (ii), due to his mathematical skills. Based at Sidcup, Kent, he spent some time located in Pollington, Yorkshire (iii), where, for a while, he was barracked in the same room as his son, Benjamin, at one point sleeping in the next bed.

Lilian started her working life working in a pencil factory in Bermondsey. She was, for many years, Secretary of the Bellingham Co-Op Women's Guild and was actively involved in organising meetings and day trips out. The Co-operative Women's Guild was a group that originated as campaigners for maternity rights and financial support for working class women and peace. They introduced the White Poppy in 1933 as a pacifist alternative to the British Legion's red poppy appeal. The Guild closed in 2016 after 133 years.

Other notable events in 1906: Edward the VII was monarch, five years after the death of Victoria, the San Francisco earthquake, HMS Dreadnought launched at Portsmouth, the first Grand Prix race in Le Mans and the Wright brothers were granted a patent for a 'flying machine'.

*Bellingham Women's Guild – a day out to Wannock Gardens in Eastbourne. Lilian is the fifth person from the left, the person to her right is Mrs Hobley, the mother of Ethel Hobley, wife of Lilians son Benjamin*

For over ten years towards the end of her life she suffered from an ulcerated leg, which involved several visits to Lewisham Hospital where she was kept in for treatment. Whenever asked how her leg was, she would reply 'it's getting better'. It never did, but such was her strength of character.

*Grangemill Road 1975, Golden Wedding Anniversary*

My grandmother, Lilian Elizabeth Howard, died on the fourteenth of November 1985 at the age of eighty-two from oesophageal cancer and was cremated at Lewisham Crematorium on the twenty-second of that month.

Alone for the first time in nearly sixty years at the age of seventy-nine and after an operation on his brain because of a severe stroke a year earlier (iv), there were concerns that Benjamin would struggle to manage. Concerns were unfounded.  He continued to live happily on his own for many years, helped by family members, until moving to Marlborough Court Care Home, in Thamesmead, London.

He died on the twenty-ninth of December 2006, 4 months into his hundredth year. The family held a party for him at the care home on his birthday. A letter from HM Queen Elizabeth II, a full life well lived and a headful of memories spanning a century and then, the Dodger was gone.

When asked once what he would like as an epitaph, he said "Mission Accomplished"

*A nice little article from the local newspaper*

## The children of Benjamin and Lilian

Benjamin, born 1927, he married Ethel Hobley, who was born in 1931. They have 3 children, Keith, Corrine and Michael. Benjamin died in 2016, Ethel at time of writing, is still alive.

Sheila Lilian, born 1930, she married Arthur Ruberry, who was born in 1919. They have 5 children, Peter, James, Susan, Pamela and Maureen. They emigrated to Australia in 1964. Arthur died in 1995; Sheila died in 2016.

Doreen Rose, born 1932, married Reginald Tidmarsh, who was born in 1930. They have 3 children, Andrew, Robert and Michael. At the time of writing, both are alive.

There are sons, daughters, grand-children and great-grandchildren both in UK and Australia – which hopefully someone will write about – one day.

## Random family photos

*Fig. 1 A young Benjamin, Shelia and Doreen*

*Fig. 2 A blustery day, a family outing with (L-R) Benjamin the younger, Doreen, Lilian, Benjamin, Sheila and Arthur Ruberry*

*Fig. 3 A nice family photo from the garden of 23 Grangemill Road, in simpler times, with children and grandchildren, taken in 1957, that's me being held by my mother, far right after my Christening at Bellingham Congregational Church. Note the small path that divided the garden, the Anderson shelter still standing – only 12 years since the end of WW2 – being used as a shed and Benjamins bike in the background, his principal mode of transport, when he wasn't walking*

## Notes:

(i)    *Alfred Sainsbury joined Sainsbury's in 1906, working at Sainsbury's head office. Prior to joining the firm, he served an apprenticeship with tea merchant George Payne, near Tower Bridge. Alfred's father, John James, saw that this training would be invaluable, as grocery buying needed different skills to the purchase of perishable goods. Subsequently, Alfred later went on to manage the grocery department, purchasing goods like tea, sugar and canned foods.*

(ii)    *During the 17th century, colonels appointed civilian agents to oversee their units' finances. In the 18th century, these civilian paymasters were provided by professional companies. It was only in 1797 that the British Army first appointed paymasters with an Army rank, initially that of captain. Other supply matters were overseen by the Board of Ordnance and then the Military Store Department, later renamed the Control Department. In 1875, the all-officer Control Department split into three. One of these sections was the Pay Sub-Department, the first ever British Army unit specifically devoted to pay matters. In 1878, the Pay Sub-Department was renamed the Army Pay Department. It was still manned entirely by officers, but in 1893 a separate Army Pay Corps was set up to provide administrative workers and clerks from among the other ranks.*

(iii)    *Pollington is a village and civil parish in the East Riding of Yorkshire, England. It is situated approximately 2 miles (3.2 km) south-west of the town of Snaith and 1 mile (1.6 km) south of the M62 motorway. It was home to RAF Snaith, a former Royal Air Force station which was located close to the village. The airfield opened 1941 before closing in 1946.*

(iv)  *Benjamin suffered a severe stroke in 1984 that resulted in a brain operation from which he recovered 98%. It was more like 100% but he complained that you could still see the hole in his head drilled as part of the operation so he marked it down!.*

# Chapter 9:
# A history of the Haymes family

I thought it relevant to include a chapter on the Haymes family as my Grandmother, Lilian Haymes was a huge influence on my cousins and me and touched so many lives with her strength and kindness.

There is a more extensive family tree compiled by my uncle, which is now in the possession of my cousin, but I have concentrated on the direct line to my grandmother.

This is a little bit of their story:

The Haymes story starts in Coventry, a city that will recur constantly in this narrative. They were part of a large amount of Warwickshire based Haymes, but to reach Bellingham, there were a lot of stopping off points. As with most family searches, scribes were more interested in the sound of a name rather than its spelling, so not until the late eighteenth century did the name Haymes appear regularly, rather than Heames and Hames.

This is a very brief resume of what I've found so far, and I've tried to add bits to build a picture, although the closer to the twentieth century we get, the more information is available.

Like all my family trees, I compiled the Haymes tree in levels, which is what I will refer to here (see Chapter 11). I was also able to embellish the tree with information I gleaned from genealogy sites by researching the Haymes specifically.

*Level 1:* The journey starts in Coventry with Thomas Howard (written in records as Heames), born in 1680, the exact date is uncertain, who met and married Rachel Horton. Rachel was born in 1682 and married Thomas on the thirty-first of January 1710 at Holy Trinity church, Coventry, in a civil ceremony, hence the lack of detailed information. Holy Trinity is a lovely grand old building which features quite often in the Haymes family.

*Fig.1 Holy Trinity church, Coventry which would have seen many Haymes baptisms, marriages and burials*

*Fig.2 Over the main internal arch is a wonderful C15th depiction of the last supper, painted after a small earthquake convinced church leaders the day of judgement was near*

Thomas and Rachel had one son that I could find, by the name of Samuel, who was born in 1716, when Rachel was thirty-four, and baptised at Holy Trinity. Within 6 years, in 1722, Rachel died at the early age of forty. Thomas outlived her by fifty-six years, dying in Coventry at the grand old age of 98. He was buried on 18th June 1778.

Other notable events in 1680: King Charles II was monarch, start of the 'penny post' delivery service, the publication of Pilgrim's Progress.

*Level 2:* Samuel, born in 1716, son of Thomas and Rachel as was customary, would have been looked after by other members of his family and by the time he was in his twenties he had met and married Sarah Burgess. Sarah was four years younger than Samuel, being born in 1720. Her family were from Kettering in Northamptonshire. They married on the seventeenth of July 1738 in Coventry. They had one son, Caleb, born in 1756 who was baptised at the Burgess family church of St Peter and St Paul, Kettering.

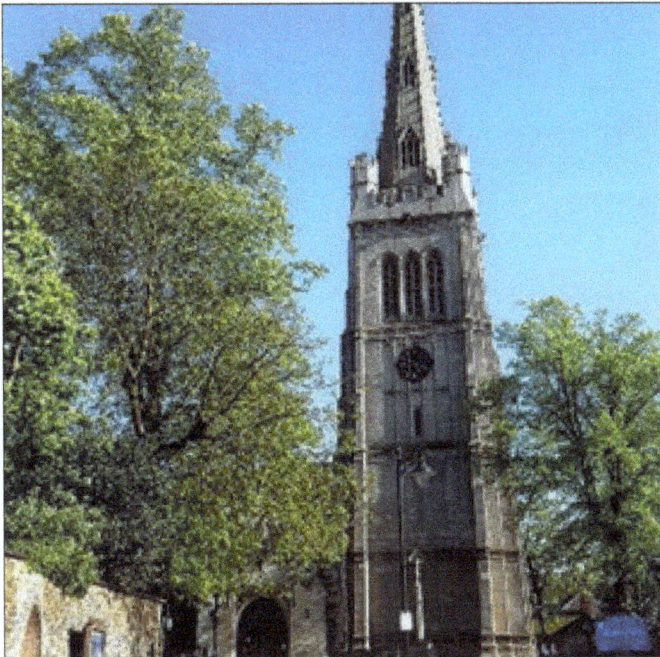

*St Peter and St Paul Kettering*

71

*The Marriage license of Caleb and Sarah*

Sarah died in 1766 at the age of 46, another early death. Samuel died in 1786 at the age of 70 so got to see his son married but never got to see his grandson, Samuel, who was born five years later.

Other notable events in 1716: George I was monarch, the beginning of the Austro-Turkish War and the Jacobite uprising.

*Level 3:* Caleb Haymes was born in Coventry on the fifteenth of May 1756, and at the age of 21 had married Sarah Essex, whose family were also from the Coventry area and who was the same age. They married at Holy Trinity on the sixth of February 1777 and had a son, Richard, on nineteenth of August 1791, when Sarah was thirty-five. But in yet another case of early death, Sarah passed away on the ninth of February 1794 at just thirty-eight, leaving the family with yet another very young child to look after.

Caleb died on the twenty-ninth of July 1838 at the age of eighty-two, continuing the pattern of Haymes women dying early and Haymes men living long lives.

Other notable events in 1756: George II was monarch, the Seven Years War with France commenced and the French invaded Minorca.

*Level 4:* Richard, born in 1791, raised by his father with the help of family members, grew up to become a watchmaker in Coventry. At the age of twenty-one he married Sarah Childs in Nuneaton, Warwickshire. Sarah was born in 1802 in Stoke, a small parish outside Coventry.

The Baptism certificate of Richard Haymes, 1791, hard to read, but a nice example of the beautiful handwriting used on these documents

## The children of Richard and Sarah:

Albert, born in 1824
Edwin, born in 1834 – my great x 2 Grandfather
Jamima, born in 1838
Emily, born in 1841

The family lived in Whitefriars Street, an old part of Coventry, leading up to what was then the White Friars monastery.

Census of 1851 – the family of Richard Haymes

Baptism certificate Sarah Childs

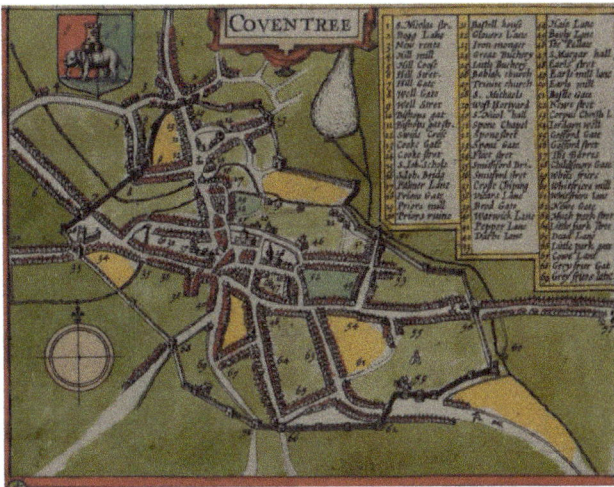

*C17th Coventry, areas 59, 60 & 61 are the Whitefriars area where the Warwickshire Haymes families lived*

Sarah's profession according to the 1851 census, was a hand loom ribbon weaver, this is the sort of machinery she would have used:

*A C19th hand operated ribbon loom, as used by Sarah. At this time, Coventry was the centre of ribbon weaving in England, with some 13,000 hand looms supported by 30,000 workers. They wove with imported fibre – the best came from Italy – after failed attempts in Britain to breed the caterpillars that produced silk fibres.*

At this point, there's an interesting turn of events. Sarah died in 1857, at the age of fifty-five. Richard would have been sixty-six. Instead of retiring and staying in Coventry, he relocated to the village of Payhembury, near Honiton in Devon. He stayed there until his death at seventy-eight on the twentieth of February 1869. He is buried in the graveyard of St Mary the Virgin parish church in Payhembury village.

*C19th Century Payhembury*

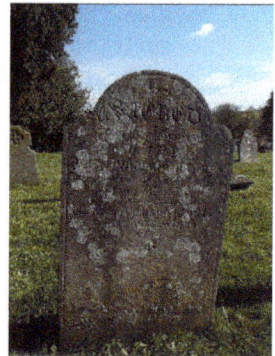

*Grave of Richard Haymes*

Other notable events in 1791: George III was monarch, the French Revolution, passing of The Constitutional Act and the first publication of The Observer newspaper.

*Level 5:* Edwin Haymes, born in 1834 was thirty-three when his mother died and didn't follow his father to Devon but stayed in Coventry for a while until relocating to Abbey Wood, in south-east London after he married. Whilst still in Coventry he married Emma Brown. She was born in 1835 in Shilton, Warwickshire, the daughter of William and Sarah Brown. They were married in a civil ceremony at Holy Trinity, Coventry in the spring of 1855.

Other notable events in 1834: William IV was monarch, the Slavery Abolition Act was passed, reform of the Poor Law, devastating fire destroys the Palace of Westminster.

*Emma Brown's profession, was Fringe Maker, creating the trimming
that was an important addition to a lady's gown – the final touch that
elevated a gown to the next level of fashion*

After their marriage they moved around quite a lot, it's difficult to keep up with them, the family home starts at Coventry, then Bethnal Green (then in Middlesex, now in east London), then Battersea, then Abbey Wood. However, just to complicate matters, Sarah, their daughter, was born or baptised in Coventry, but her two elder brothers were born in Bethnal Green, whilst her five younger siblings were born in Battersea. Edwin was a Tailor by profession, so his skills were transferrable from one area to another, Emma's skills, however, were particular to the Coventry area.

There was quite a large family to move around, with eight children, nearly all of which became Tailors by trade.

*The formidable looking Mr Edwin Haymes, looking very much the Dickensian villain here. One didn't smile for the camera in those days*

## The children of Edwin and Emma:

Arthur, born in Bethnal Green in 1855

Richard, born in Bethnal Green in 1856

Sarah, born in Coventry (although this could have been the place of baptism) in 1860

Martin, born in Battersea in 1866

Myra, born in Battersea in 1868

Burman, born in Battersea in 1872, my great Grandfather

Lemuel, born in Battersea in 1877

Miriam, born in Battersea in 1879

Edwin ended his travels in Abbey Wood and died in 1904 at the age of 70, Emma outlived him by eleven years and died in 1915 at the age of 80.

*Level 6:* Burman Cassaw Haymes, born in Battersea in 1872, at that time in the county of Surrey. A tailor by trade, like his father and most of his siblings. After his apprenticeship, he worked in a shop in Bermondsey, where he seems to have specialised in military tailoring, and it's here that the Howards and the Haymes start to move closer.

It was while he was working in Bermondsey that he met Eliza Milford, the woman who would become his wife and my maternal great Grandmother.

Eliza was born in 1875, she was the daughter of Charles Milford, a joiner from Collumpton in Devon, who was born in 1843 and Elizabeth Ann Milford (nee Conland), who was born in Shoreditch, east London a few years earlier in 1839. Somehow, their paths crossed in Yorkshire, where they lived in the tiny fishing village of Skinningrove in North Yorkshire *(fig 1)* and raised three children, Elizabeth, James and Eliza. The family are recorded as living in different addresses around Yorkshire when the children are young.

However, Elizabeth died at the early age of forty-seven, in Goole, Yorkshire. Eliza is only eleven years old when this happens. Charles was 43 and decides to relocate to Bermondsey and takes Eliza with him. Charles died in Bermondsey in 1928 at the age of eighty-five. Eliza stayed in Bermondsey with her father and would probably have passed a Howard or two on her travels, had she known it.

*Fig.1 Skinningrove, a small quiet costal village in North Yorkshire, home to the Milford family*

Back to Burman Cassaw Haymes, currently working as a Tailor in Bermondsey, who meets and eventually marries Eliza Milford. They married on the sixteenth of July 1900 at St. George the Martyr church in Queen Street, Holborn, London. Burman was twenty-six and Eliza was twenty-four. They lived in Earlsfield, near Battersea before moving to Leyton in Essex and then to 31 Palmerston Road in Plumstead, south-east London. This address remained the family home until the move to 34 Kipling Street in Bermondsey, an address that is a firm fixture in the history of both families.

*St George the Martyr, Holborn*

*Marriage certificate of Burman and Eliza, witnessed by Edwin Haymes and Charles Milford. The Registrar had problems with Burman's name*

1911 census, Palmerston Road, Plumstead, the Haymes family, Burman, Eliza, Charles, Elizabeth & Lilian. The youngest daughter, Winnifred wasn't born, but the census includes a boarder, Emma Haymes, Burman's mother-in-law

Fig.1 Burman Cassaw Haymes

Fig.2 Eliza Haymes, holding my mother, next to her is her youngest daughter, Winnifred (Win), my great Aunt, she is holding my mother's elder sister, Sheila

Eliza's profession was 'sewing machinist' but she worked as an office cleaner in a tea warehouse and a butter warehouse, near London Bridge. She was always to be seen in an apron. My mother remembers her as a lovely, generous person, but very poor. She lived with Benjamin and Lilian at Grangemill Road in her later years.

Burman died in 1940 at the age of 68, Eliza died in 1961 at the age of 86, their eldest daughter, Lilian would become my maternal grandmother and would marry Benjamin Howard, which is where the connection of the Howards and Haymes starts and becomes the final phase of this Chapter.

Eliza became ill towards the end of her life; at that time she lived alone in a small flat in Bermondsey. Two men living in the upstairs flat used to look after her but when she became too ill, my grandmother moved her into the family home at Grangemill Road. I suspect she also had a touch of dementia as she had a habit of wandering off, once getting lost for so long a small search party of neighbours had to go out and find her. Close to Grangemill Road, across a railway track as I recall, there was a small recreation ground which I used to walk over to, which is where they eventually found her. There's a story that she left the house early in the morning once, dressed in black with her hair up and scared the life out of the paper boy! After a few years she was well enough to return home but not able to look after herself, so was taken into a care home where she spent the rest of her days. When talking to my mother about her, she always comments on how lovely and kind she was. Even sixty-five years after her death, people remember her with fondness, which is quite a legacy.

Other notable events in 1872: Victoria was monarch, the first FIFA recognised football match between England and Scotland was played and the first edition of Chambers English Dictionary was published.

## *Level 7:* **The children of Burman and Eliza**

Charles Edwin Haymes, he was born in 1902 but died very young in 1935 at the age of thirty-three. He was born in Leyton, Essex and married Rose Garrett (1905 – 1986). Rose was thirty when Charles died, she remarried four years later, and her surname was Marsh in the 1939 census. She died in Southwark in 1986 at the age of eighty. Charles was my grandmother's favourite, and his death had a profound effect on her for the rest of her life.

Lilian Elizabeth Haymes (Sissy), my grandmother, born in Leyton and whose history is covered in Chapter 7

Elizabeth Haymes was born in Leyton in 1906 and had mental health problems. She was confined to various mental institutions in London before going to Leavesden Hospital, near Watford when it was taken over by the LCC (London County Council). It's still in operation, managed by the NHS. She ended her days there and died in 1986 at the age of eighty.

Maurice Haymes, born 1907 in Plumstead, who married Louie Beatrice Gaywood, who was born in 1909. Maurice died in 1961 at the age of fifty-four, Louie died in 2006 at the age of 97. She lived on the same estate as my grandmother and we visited her regularly, she was a wonderful woman and was affectionately known as 'Aunt Lou'. She continued the tradition of referring to my grandmother by her nickname of 'Sissy'.

Winnifred Mary (Win), born in Bermondsey in 1912, she was a nurse and not widely liked by the rest of the family for reasons I am unaware of. On the census of 1939 she used the surname Vangilder. She married a David Vangilder in 1942. She died in 1978 at the age of sixty-six. David Vangilder outlived her by 26 years and died in 2004 at the age of 92 as a resident of Queens Oak care home in Peckham, south London.

*An elegantly posed, undated photo of my grandmother,*
*Lilian Haymes*

# Chapter 10:
# Howard Family Tree

William Howard 1776 - 1838

Mary Ann Reader 1792 - 1852

James Howard 1817 -

Elizabeth Dunckley 1809 - 1878

William James Howard 1847 - 1926

Caroline Davis 1847 - 1921

Harriet Maria Howard 1849 -

Sophia Howard 1850

Eliza Howard 1852 -

James Howard 1840 -

Fanny Emily Howard 1842 -

Elizabeth Howard 1845 -

Mary Ann Howard 1889 -

Emily Catherine Howard 1869 - 1937

William Henry Howard (2) 1869 - 1937

Catherine Elizabeth Howard 1872 -

Henry Alfred Howard 1874 -

Benjamin Harwood Howard 1883 - 1964

Sarah Ann (Frances) Martin 1883 - 1930

Joseph Dunckley Howard 1878 - 1936

Samuel Davis Howard 1879 - 1960

George Edward Howard 1880 -

Thomas Robinso Howard 1884 -

Annie Howard 1886 -

John Wheeler Howard 1889 -

Benjamin Howard 1906 - 2006

Lilian Elizabeth Haynes 1903 - 1985

Doreen Rose Howard 1932 -

Reginald Stanley Tidmarsh 1930 - 2025

Rose Lilian Kirk 1908 - 1989

Thomas Howard 1906 - 2006

Catherine Howard 1935 - 1989

Alfred Howes 1935 - 1971

Arthur Bertram Rubery 1919 - 1995

Sheila Lilian Howard 1940 - 2016

Ethel Holley 1931 - 2025

Benjamin Howard 1937 - 2016

# Chapter 11:
# Haymes Family Tree

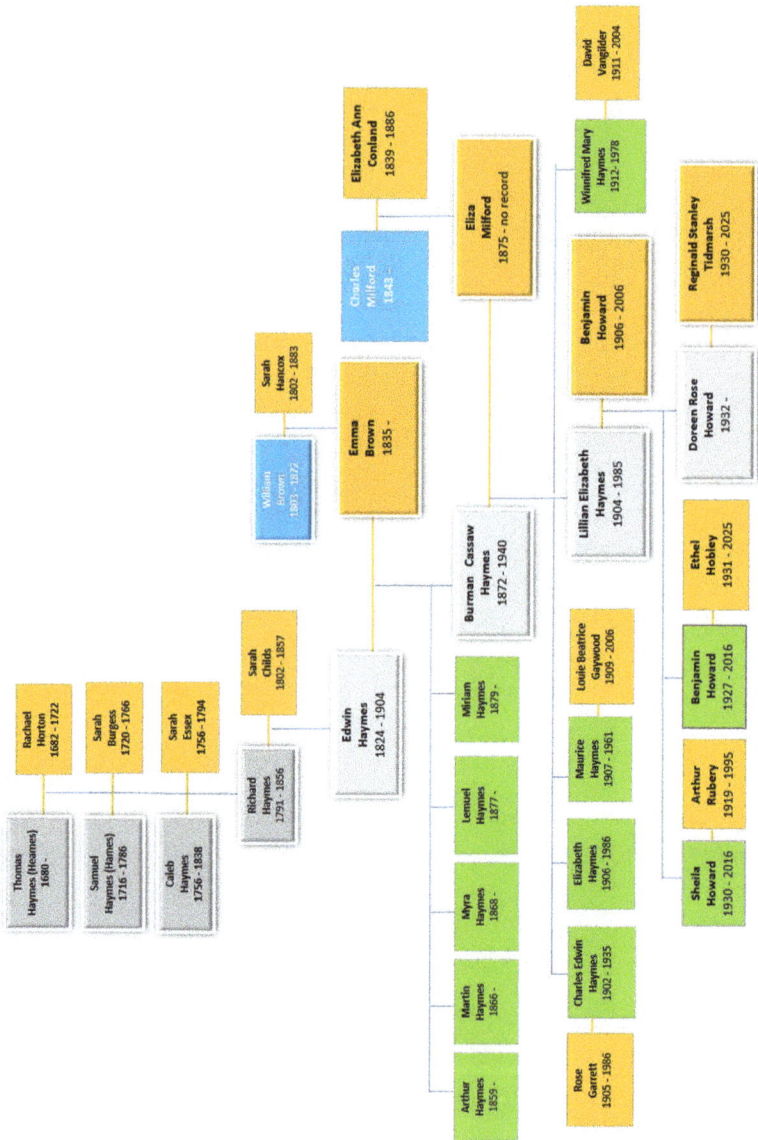

Elizabeth Ann Conland 1839 - 1886

David Vangilder 1911 - 2004

Winnifred Mary Haymes 1912 - 1978

Reginald Stanley Tidmarsh 1930 - 2025

Charles Milford 1843 -

Eliza Milford 1875 - no record

Benjamin Howard 1906 - 2006

Sarah Hancox 1802 - 1883

Emma Brown 1835 -

William Brown 1803 - 1872

Doreen Rose Howard 1932 -

Lillian Elizabeth Haymes 1904 - 1985

Rachael Horton 1682 - 1722

Sarah Burgess 1720 - 1766

Sarah Essex 1756 - 1794

Sarah Childs 1802 - 1857

Burman Cassaw Haymes 1872 - 1940

Ethel Hobley 1931 - 2025

Richard Haymes 1791 - 1856

Edwin Haymes 1824 - 1904

Miriam Haymes 1879 -

Louie Beatrice Gaywood 1909 - 2006

Benjamin Howard 1927 - 2016

Thomas Haymes (Heames) 1680 -

Samuel Haymes (Hames) 1715 - 1786

Caleb Haymes 1756 - 1838

Lemuel Haymes 1877 -

Maurice Haymes 1907 - 1961

Arthur Rubery 1919 - 1995

Myra Haymes 1868 -

Elizabeth Haymes 1906 - 1986

Sheila Howard 1930 - 2016

Martin Haymes 1866 -

Charles Edwin Haymes 1902 - 1935

Arthur Haymes 1859 -

Rose Garrett 1905 - 1986

# Chapter 12:
# Spitalfields Market
### For 47 years, the workplace of my Grandfather

Located in the heart of London's east end, the Spitalfields area features in the stories of Charles Dickens and was a hunting ground for Jack the Ripper. The area took its name from St Mary Spittel, a former priory and hospital. A market has been here since 1682, when Charles II granted a Charter for a market on Thursdays and Saturdays. Eventually expanding to six days a week, the area attracted many cultures and artisans and fed London's growing demand for fruit and vegetables. Work on the new market started in 1876 and it was extended in 1920, when Benjamin started working there. It was relocated to Leyton in 1991 and is now a tourist attraction housing artisan businesses.

In the last eighteen months of the Fruit & Vegetable Market in Spitalfields, young photographers Mark Jackson & Huw Davies set out to record the life of the market that operated on this site for over three centuries, before it closed forever in 1991. Here is a small selection that I think best display the atmosphere of the market at the time my grandfather worked there. To me, the photos transcend imagery and create the sounds and smells that grandad would have experienced from his small office as he updated both accounting ledgers – one for the firm, one for the taxman.

An albeit brief glimpse into another world, one that knew my Grandfather.

*Acknowledgement: Spitalfields Life*

*An etching from 1842*

*Still busy in the 1990's before closing and
moving to Leyton*

*To mark the rebuilding in 1887,
the year of Victoria's jubilee*

*The old market reborn*

*The market, looking east reflected in two eras*

*A letter from Mr Wakefield confirming Benjamins release from
Army service and the hope of his speedy return to work*

*All that's left of the Wakefield office at 108 Commercial Street,*
*where Benjamin worked*

# Chapter 13:
# Co-operative Women's Guild

The Co-operative Women's Guild was an auxiliary organization of the co-operative movement in the United Kingdom.

*Founder Alice Acland*

*Bellingham branch presentation*

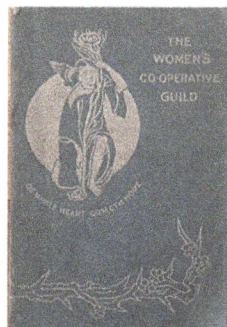

*"Of whole heart, cometh hope"*

The guild was founded in 1883 by Alice Acland, who edited the "Women's Corner" of the *Co-operative News,* and Mary Lawrenson, a teacher who suggested the creation of an organization to promote instructional and recreational classes for mothers and girls. Acland began organizing a Women's League for the Spread of Co-operation, which held its first formal meeting of 50 women at the 1883 Co-operative Congress in Edinburgh and established local branches. It began as an organization dedicated to spreading the co-operative movement, but soon expanded beyond the retail-based focus of the movement to organizing political campaigns on women's issues including health and suffrage. Annie Williams, a suffragette organiser for the Women's Social and Political Union in Newcastle found in 1910 that "Co-operative women are very keen to know about 'Votes for Women'."

In 1884, the League changed its name to the Women's Co-operative Guild and later to the Co-operative Women's Guild and by 1910, it had 32,000 members. Maternity benefits were included in the National Insurance Act 1911 because of the guild's pressure. The guild became more politically active, and expanded its work beyond the British Isles; their objectives included the establishment of minimum wages and maternity benefits, and in April 1914 they were involved in an International Women's Congress at The Hague, which passed a resolution totally opposing war:

After World War I, the guild became more involved in peace activism, concentrating especially on the social and political conditions that encouraged or gave rise to war, as well as opposition to the arms trade. In 1933 they introduced the White Poppy as a pacifist alternative to the British Legion's annual red poppy appeal. (Note the two white poppies on the banner). At its peak, the guild had 1,500 branches and 72,000 members.

The guild continued with several local branches, although it did not have the visibility within the Co-operative movement that it once did. It closed after 133 years on 25 June 2016.

# Chapter 14:
## A few memories

**A collection of things I found along the way. By no means extensive, but, for me, each piece captures a moment in time.**

Benjamin was famous for phrases that stay in the mind of those that heard them. Here is a selection, some readers may need some interpretation.

- I can remember when oranges were 38 for a shilling
- Everybody's buying these big potatoes, we used to call them 'lumps' in the market and used to throw them away because we couldn't sell them for half a crown a hundredweight
- Those little sprouts are now a delicacy, in my day the farmer used to plough them in
- The women in the supermarket pile everything into one trolley and have no idea of prices – they ought to go into another supermarket to check the prices
- I can remember when German banknotes were a penny each
- One day, at the day care centre he attended he was given a cup of tea with hardly any milk, to which he commented: "I see the old cows died!"

## A poem, written by my father on the death of Benjamin at 100

'Great Great Grandad Howard'

Benjamin Howard, now deceased and from this mortal coil released

Can now in spirit rise above and live in peace with joy and love

Amongst those who have gone before, to that far and distant shore

Where pain and sorrow are not known, and great vegetables are grown

There he can roll up his sleeves and dig and hoe and rake and sieve

And in that very fertile ground, grow runner beans
worth a pound a pound

For in this life, he was quite sure, that they would be
that price, and more

After blending tea for the pre-Lord Sainsbury

He realised at twenty-three this was not the life for he

And to Spitalfields did go where in with Wakefields his lot throw

There he spent his working life, apart from the second world war strife

When the Government insisted, into the Pay Corp he would be enlisted

And when he had won the war, well him and another few million more

Back to the market he gladly went, where the rest of
his working life he spent

Rising early in the morn' setting out at the crack of dawn

But before and every day, a full English breakfast, then on his way

Into the garden, after work, never did dear old Ben shirk

There to tend his flowers and veg' and cut the grass and privet hedge

It was left to us to know the sands of time were running low

One thing shone throughout the tears –

OLD BEN HAD MADE A HUNDRED YEARS

But this is sadly in the past – nothing good can ever last

Other than, you will agree, forever in our memory

Reginald S Tidmarsh

95

Lilian was a prolific letter writer and my uncles' files contain some of the letters she sent him when he was away in the Army. It was the only real form of communication for most people at that time. In this instant world we live in, it's difficult to remember the thrill of receiving a letter from a loved one. If you remember Lilian and close your eyes, you can her voice reading it. If nothing else, it takes one back to darker, or maybe just different times.

**This letter was typed by my uncle Benny, from a letter he received from his Mum, Lilian. Note that she couldn't get any cake, the apples weren't worth buying and that she was saving her fruit ration for a Christmas pudding:**

A LETTER FROM MY MUM

23 Grangemill Road

Thursday

My Dear Benny,

Glad to receive your letter yesterday. I don't know what to send you in the way of cake as I cant find any fruit cake and if I send a jam sponge I am afraid it will get squashed so I am sending some biscuits and some bath buns. Doreen was with me at the time I bought them and she said it was because you eat them in the bath. Doreen hasn't been to school for a fortnight as she hasn't been very well. I wont be able to make any bread pudding for a while as I am saving my fruit for a Xmas pudding. I will make one for you as well as some mince pies. I hope the trousers fit you, if they are too long just brace them up. I hope you will be able to buy a pair of football boots cheap Daddy will pay, if not we will get you a pair later on, and we will fetch the gum boots down with us. I told Mrs Colenutt about Cliff, she was just sending a parcel to him. I didn't get any apples and Daddy said they weren't worth buying, but I managed to get you an orange but don't forget to save the orange peel it will go into the Christmas pudding as we cant get any lemons. We have another rabbit now, that makes three, Daddy has made two hutches and Doreen talks to them like babies. Save all your bits a pieces for the rabbits anything you don't want on your allotment.
Well son this is all for now so cheerio till next Suday
With love from your loving Mum and Dad

xx

# From Lilian to 'Benny', note the reference to her brother Maurice

**A wonderful little letter, just a catch up and a quick chat between mother and son, separated by circumstances outside of their control**

Lilian wrote to BBC radio children's hour ("on a postcard please") for all her grandchildren's birthdays' and always took pleasure in telling us which record she had requested. As far as I know, none of her requests were ever played, but that's not really the point.

# The death certificates of Benjamin and Lilian

**CERTIFIED COPY**
Pursuant to the Births and

**OF AN ENTRY**
Deaths Registration Act 1953

## DEATH

| | Entry No. 50 |
|---|---|
| Registration district Bexley | Administrative area |
| Sub-district Bexley | London Borough of Bexley |

1. Date and place of death
   Twenty-ninth December 2006
   Marlborough Court Nursing Home, Copperfield Road, Thamesmead

| 2. Name and surname | 3. Sex Male |
|---|---|
| Benjamin HOWARD | 4. Maiden surname of woman who has married |

5. Date and place of birth
   5th July 1906      Bermondsey Southwark

6. Occupation and usual address
   Vegetable Salesman (retired) Widower of Lillian HOWARD
   Marlborough Court Nursing Home, Copperfield Road, Thamesmead SE28

| 7(a) Name and surname of informant | (b) Qualification |
|---|---|
| Benjamin HOWARD | Son |

(c) Usual address
   4 Whitehaven Court, 22 Crook Log, Bexleyheath, Kent

8. Cause of death
   I (a) Senescence

   II  Hypertension

   Certified by   A Milstein MB

9. I certify that the particulars given by me above are true to the best of my knowledge and belief
   B Howard                                                                    Signature of informant

| 10. Date of registration | 11. Signature of registrar |
|---|---|
| Third January 2007 | Graham A Dalton Registrar |

Certified to be a true copy of an entry in a register in my custody.

GrahA Dalton {      *Superintendent Registrar      Date 3.1, 2007
                    *Registrar
                    *Strike out whichever does not apply

## CERTIFIED COPY of an ENTRY OF DEATH

Issued at a reduced fee in pursuance of and for the purposes of the First Schedule to the
INDUSTRIAL ASSURANCE AND FRIENDLY SOCIETIES ACT 1948
and the Fifth Schedule to the FRIENDLY SOCIETIES ACT 1974

| DEATH | | Entry No. | 240 |
|---|---|---|---|

Registration district **LEWISHAM** LONDON BOROUGH OF **LEWISHAM** Administrative area

Sub-district **LEWISHAM**

1. Date and place of death  Fourteenth November 1985
   Lewisham Hospital, Lewisham

2. Name and surname  Lillian Elizabeth HOWARD

3. Sex  Female

4. Maiden surname of woman who has married  HAYMES

5. Date and place of birth  23rd September 1903
   Bermondsey, Southwark

6. Occupation and usual address  Wife of Benjamin HOWARD Fruit salesman (retired)
   28 Grangemill Road, SE6

7. (a) Name and surname of informant  Benjamin HOWARD
   (b) Qualification  Son
   (c) Usual address  8 Hythe Avenue, Bexleyheath, Kent

8. Cause of death  1a Haemorrhage
   b Carcinoma of oesophagus
   Certified by A Gordon Davies Coroner for Inner South London after post mortem without inquest

9. I certify that the particulars given by me above are true to the best of my knowledge and belief
   B. Howard
   Signature of informant

10. Date of registration  Fifteenth November 1985

11. Signature of registrar  [signature] Deputy Registrar

Certified to be a true copy of an entry in a register in my custody.
[signature] Registrar  15. 11. 1985. Date

Person to whom issued  Name and surname (in full)  BENJAMIN HOWARD
Address  8 Hythe Avenue, Bexleyheath, Kent

Relationship to deceased: child, stepchild or grandchild (delete those inapplicable).

Note: Child includes a child who has been adopted by order of a court under the Adoption Acts in England and Wales, Scotland, Northern Ireland, the Isle of Man, or any of the Channel Islands, or one of the countries or territories listed in the Schedule to the Adoptions (Designation of Overseas Adoptions) Order 1973.

CAUTION:—Any person who (1) falsifies any of the particulars on this certificate or (2) uses a falsified certificate as true, knowing it to be false, is liable to prosecution.

ED 558136

*Benjamin Howard*

*Lilian Elizabeth Howard*

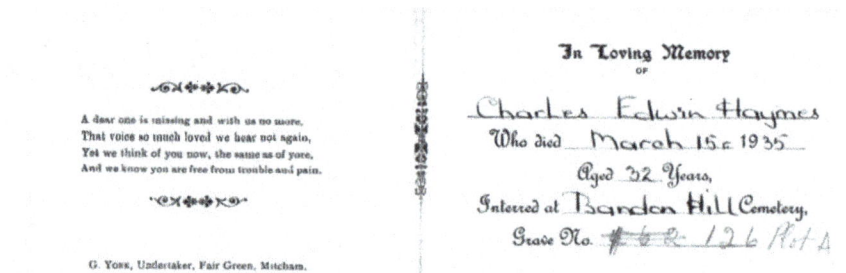

*Fig.1 A small card from the memorial service of Lilian's brother, my great Uncle Charles. He was her favourite, and it broke her heart when he died tragically young at 32. Those who enjoy gravestone hunting as much as I do will appreciate the importance of the plot and grave number.*

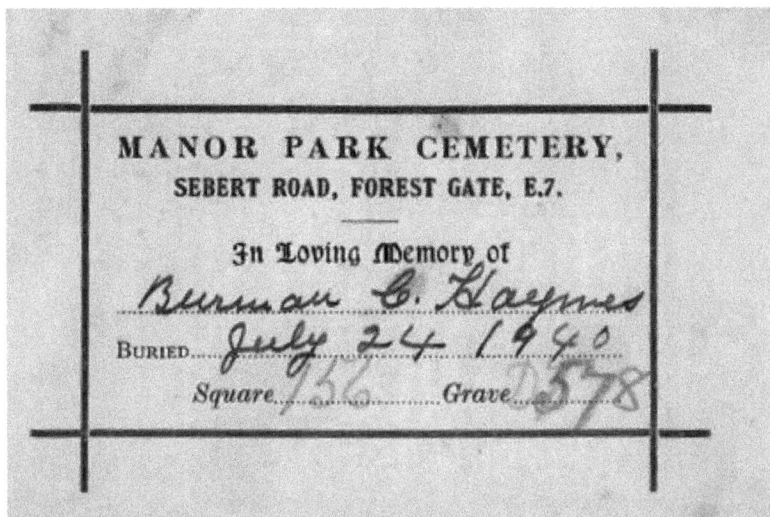

MANOR PARK CEMETERY,
SEBERT ROAD, FOREST GATE, E.7.

In Loving Memory of

*Burman C. Haymes*

BURIED *July 24 1940*

Square *756* Grave *D578*

*Fig.2 A small card from the burial service of Lilian's father, my great Grandfather, Burman Cassaw Haymes and again, the plot and grave number to add some intrigue. I have tried to find the source of the names Burman and Cassaw, both very unusual names, but so far to no avail*

*Fig.3 The garden at 23 Grangemill Road was a work of logistical genius. Every spare inch was filled with something. There were always dozens of old tobacco tins containing runner bean seeds for the next season. When you walked out of the backdoor, there was an open-fronted storeroom, repurposed from the old Anderson shelter, a small patch of grass for my grandmother and then an expanse of flowers and vegetation, with my grandfather invariably plodding away at something out there*

*Fig.4 This is a rare gem of a photo as it's the only one I can find with Benjamin's sister, Catherine (commonly called 'Kate'), my great Aunt. Taken in the back yard of Kipling Street: (From L-R) Rear, Benjamin and Kate. Sitting, Lilian, Frances and a young Benjamin (son of Benjamin). If you look closely, the neighbours are looking over the fence. This photo really catches a moment, there's a joke being shared, possibly the photographer noticed the heads in the background. The yard is surrounded by rabbit hutches and note Lilian's hat perched on top of one*

*Fig.5 Another interesting find, this is a rare photo of Maurice, Lilian's younger brother, and Louie Beatrice Gaywood, or 'Lou' as she was affectionately known*

Fig.6 Kipling Street figures prominently in the story of both families, I enclosed
a picture in the book of the street in the 1900's when the families would have
known it before the move to Bellingham. However, I thought it was a little sanitised,
so I have included this photo taken from the back of the buildings to show how
squalid conditions were

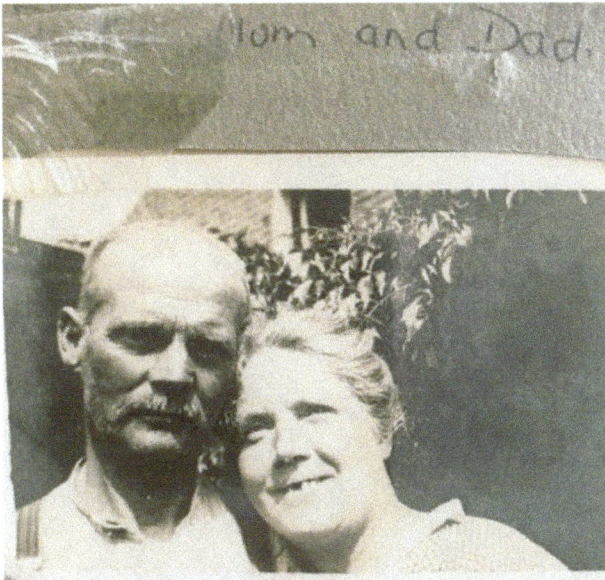

Fig.7 'Mum and Dad' from my mother's collection. Not much else to say really

*Fig.8 A day at the beach for Lilian's brother, my great uncle Charles and his wife, my great aunt Rose. Charles was Lilian's favourite brother and when he died young, in his thirties, it broke her heart and she never really recovered*

*Fig.9 A photo of a young great uncle Maurice, Lilian's brother*

*Fig.10 Benjamin and his granddaughter, my cousin, Susan Hobbs (nee Rubery) on a visit from Australia, taken with Benjamin at 23 Grangemill Road, note the signature headgear and one of his beloved newspapers, from which he collected cartoons anecdotes and odd pieces of news*

*Fig.11 Family gatherings at Christmas, the black & white photo would be at least 60 years ago, the colour photo far more recent, only around 50 years ago, followed by some more recent photos in both UK and Australia. The Rubery side of the family recently celebrated 60 years in Australia*

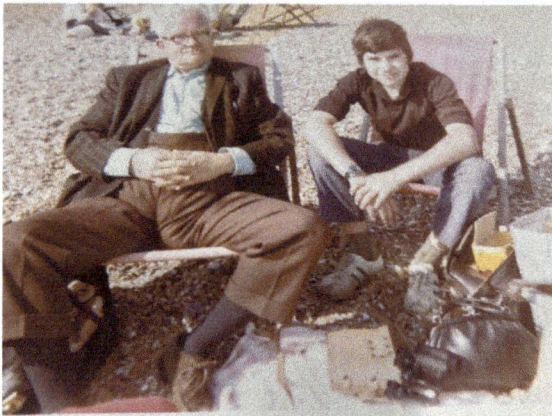

*Fig.12 A family day out at the beach, probably taken around 1971. Grandad Howard and me watching the world go by. With thanks to my brother Robert, who found this and sent it to me. I don't remember this day, but, in a way, I do. The more one looks at an old photo, the more one remembers*

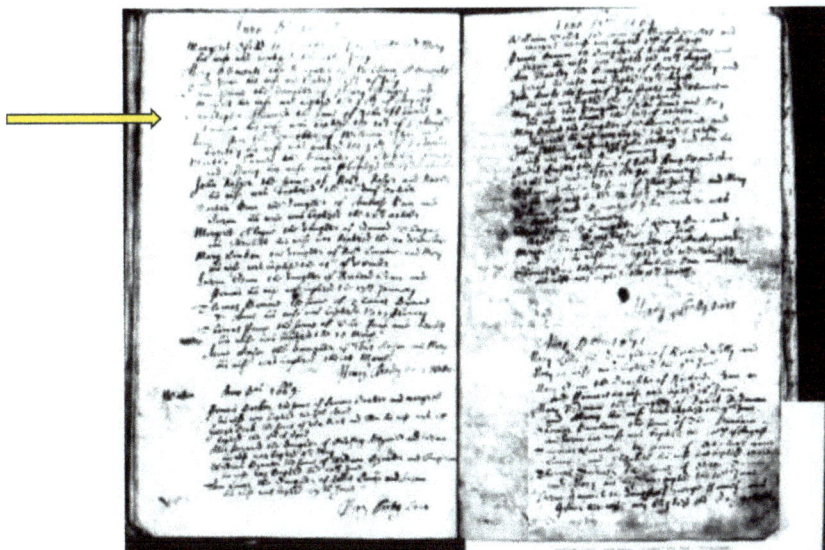

*Baptism of Christopher Howard, my great x 7 grandfather at*
*St Mary's Watton, Norfolk, 1668*

*Birth certificate of William James Howard, my gt x 2 grandfather,*
*on the 15th of January 1847*

*A certified copy of the marriage certificate of my great x2 grandparents on 27th July 1868 at St John the Baptist, Margate, Kent*

*Burial of Thomas Haymes (Heames) 18th June 1778 at the age of 98*

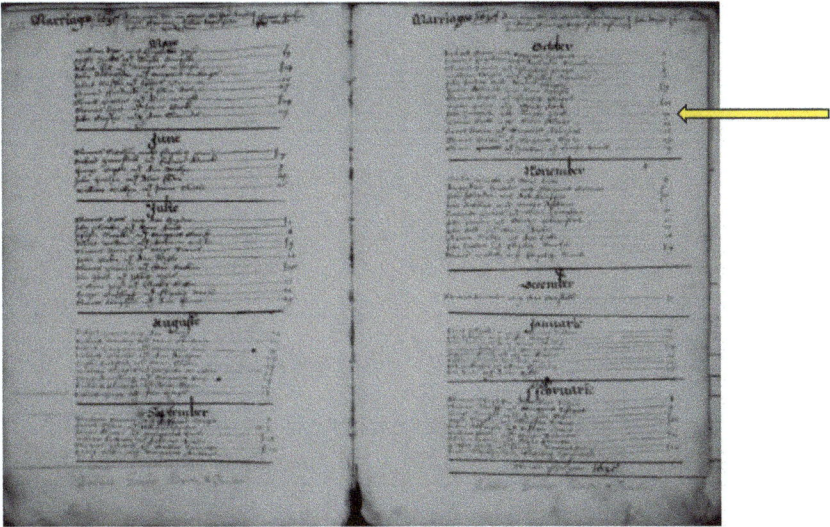

*Marriage record of my great x 9 grandparents, John Howard and Susan Becke, on the 19th October 1635. Note the Old English writing on the tops of the pages*

*I believe this to be my great x 8 grandmother, Hannah Daroch from Wingham in Somerset*

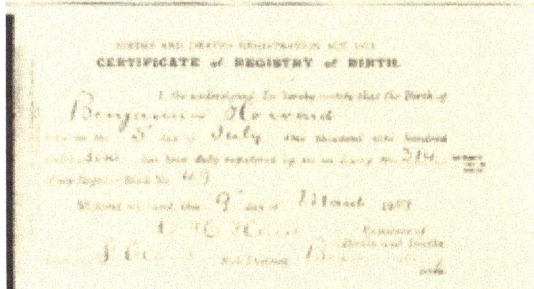

*Dodgers' Birth certificate, 1906*

111

*1939 Census – Benjamin Howard – managing salesman, Lilian – unpaid domestic duties, no children at no 23, they had all been evacuated*

*Register of birth, Doreen Rose Howard, mothers name misspelt as Haynes (3rd from bottom, LH side)*

*London School Board, admission no. 7221, Benjamin Howard, who left Galleywall Road school 22.07.1920 at 14 to work*

## Youthful photos of the children of Benjamin and Lilian

*Benjamin*          *Sheila Lilian*          *Doreen Rose*

# "All about him", an excerpt from my Uncle's grandparents' book about his father.

## BEN HOWARD          All about him

Born at Lynton Road, Bermondsey on 5th July 1906, Lived in the area, just off the Old Kent Road for about 20 years. Had one brother Tom and a sister Kate, long since deceased. He went to infants school at Monnow Road, Bermondsey and Senior School at Galleywall Road, Bermondsey. He wanted to go on to further education but was forced to go to work at 14.

His first job was at George Paynes the Tea Merchants at Tower Bridge. He started as a tea boy. He was a tea boy with a difference, he had to boil the water for the tea tasting, if it wasn't absolutely correct he had to make another dozen cups. He was particularly proud of the fact that Mr Alfred Sainsbury, when buying his tea, regularly came to have a chat with him. He worked there for four years and then as a salesman and secretary for a Pea and Potato company in Spitalfields Market for 47 years.

He married Lillian on Boxing Day 1926,at St Annes Church in Bermondsey and had 3 children , Ben, Sheila and Doreen
He lived for some years in Southwark and Bermondsey and in 1938 moved to Bellingham Estate, Lewisham. A move he had worked hard for.
He lived there for 70 years.

In 1984 he had a severe stroke that resulted in a brain operation. He 98% recovered. The other 2% was his complaint that you could still see the hole that had been drilled in his head.!

How has he lived so long? Every morning at 4 o'clock his wife Lillian cooked him an enormous breakfast, fried in beef dripping!

In retirement he was well known for his favourite sayings –
         "Those little sprouts and flat peas are now a delicacy, in my day the farmer would plough them in."
         "Every one is buying these large potatoes, in my day we called them lumps and couldn't sell them for half a crown a hundredweight!"

         He was called up in 1944 and went into the Army Pay Corps,  In April 1945 when Ben senior was stationed in Oldham and Ben junior was at a village in Yorkshire he got a lift over there and for one night they slept in adjoining beds in the same barrack room.

One of his main occupations during his long retirement was tending his garden. He regularly planted 200 runner bean seeds every year, saving the seeds from one year to the next. He also filled 2 scrapbooks a week. He made wooden containers with a handle and painted them different colours
He always said that the words on his tombstone should be MISSION ACCOMPLISHED.

*Benjamin Howard, as his grandchildren remember him, in his garden,
signature woolly hat, keeping busy, singing, whistling, dispensing wisdom,
making things grow as he reflected on an ever-changing world*

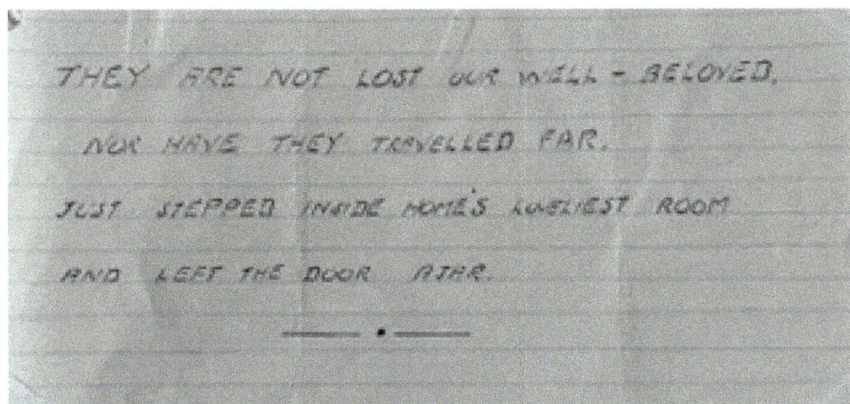

THEY ARE NOT LOST OUR WELL - BELOVED,

NOR HAVE THEY TRAVELLED FAR.

JUST STEPPED INSIDE HOME'S LOVELIEST ROOM

AND LEFT THE DOOR AJAR.

*Epitaph, written by my grandfather, Benjamin, at the age of 96 in his own hand*

# The red light

SE.6.

10th October 1958.

Sir,

It has been reported that, on the 5th October 1958, when you were { driving / propelling } a vehicle at Bromley Road, Catford, SE.6,

you failed to conform to the indication given by an authorised traffic sign.

No further action will be taken in regard to this matter, but I am to inform you that, if you are reported again, it may be necessary to take proceedings against you in respect of the later case.

I am, Sir, Your obedient Servant,

*Chief Superintendent.*

To Mr. Benjamin HOWARD,

23, Grangemill Road,

CATFORD, SE.6.

M.P.-44275/5,000 Mar./1951 w96 (2)

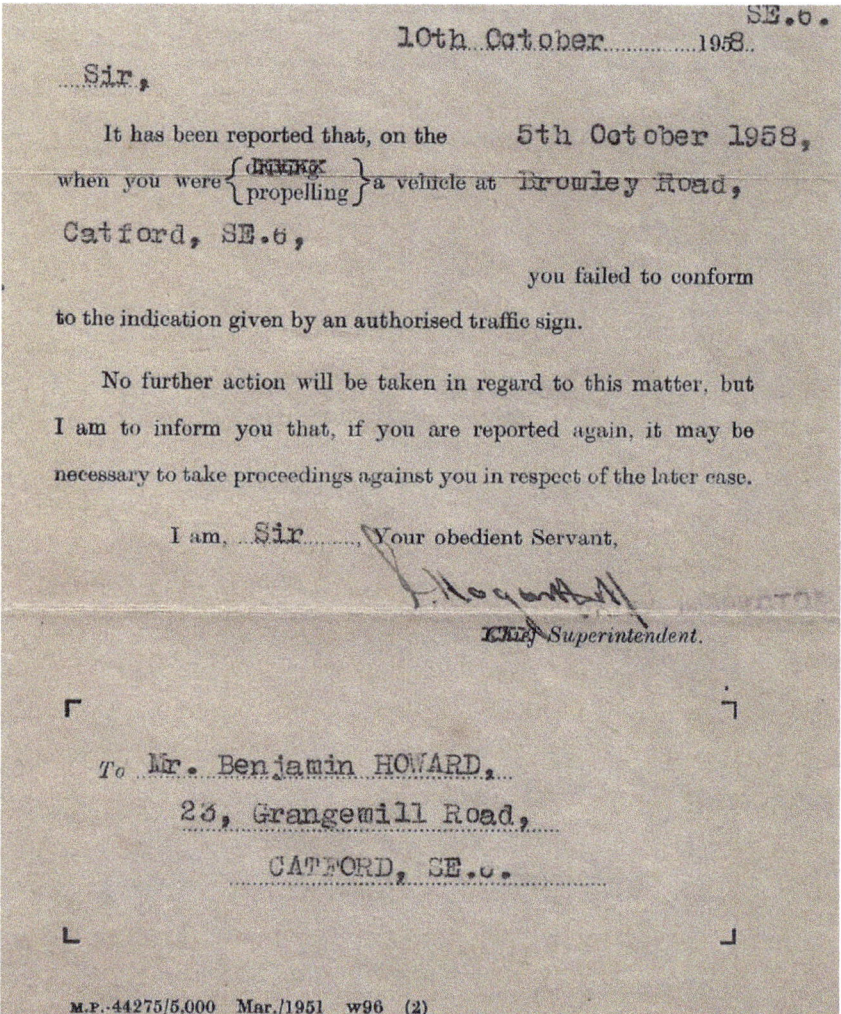

*October 1958, Dodger was caught riding his bike through a red light and let off with a warning, good job they didn't know about the Fire Wardens hose!*

# Afterword

The essence of researching family histories is that you have the chance to reflect on the importance of family lines and legacies. This photo, sent to me by my cousin has a nice little story attached to it. Many years ago, my grandfather Benjamin expressed a wish to his son, my uncle, that, down the family line, the eldest son would have Benjamin included in their name.

This photo, taken in 1996, shows four generations of Howards, all with Benjamin in their names. At the time of being taken, the four generations in this photo spanned 90 years. This year, 2025, will cover a span of 142 years since the birth of my great Grandfather, Benjamin Harwood Howard in 1883. The legacy of naming sons Benjamin has continued with my cousin Keith's son, Daniel Benjamin, continuing a tradition that hopefully will continue as a testament to the long line of Howards that bought us to this point.

*Father & son*

Families, by their very nature, encapsulate memories and emotions some exposed, some hidden but all are part of the legacy left to us by our ancestors. The Howards and Haymes families are no exception, and I hope that one day someone will decide that maybe it's a good idea to continue the story.

# Appendix 1 – The Bellingham Estate

After the squalor and deprivation of Deptford and Bermondsey, the Howard family moved into the relatively new estate built on land in Bellingham by the London County Council (LCC), an estate that was a new concept at the time providing new, modern housing and green spaces for working class Londoners.

The land for the Bellingham Estate (Bellingham Farm and part of White House Farm) was bought in 1920, and building of the main estate was completed in 1923. Historical names were chosen for the roads. Some related to King Alfred, who was thought to have been lord of the manor of Lewisham. My paternal grandparents lived at 1 King Alfred Avenue, a ten-minute walk to the Howard's house at 23 Grangemill Road.

In more recent times the designation 'council estate' acquired many negative associations, but the Bellingham Council estate of my childhood and of my parents was quite another: "It was a large sprawling village of cottagey houses of varying styles and sizes arranged along tree lined avenues and crescents and pleasant greens. The houses had back gardens tended with great devotion, and in the islands of land behind some of the rows of back-gardens from adjoining streets were allotments. The small front gardens were hedged with dark green privet and the identical half glazed front doors were painted in a limited range of standard colours. This uniformity, far from turning the estate into a flat repetitive landscape, worked to bind together the delightful variety and orientation of the houses built of red and yellow brick into an attractive village. What could have been an exercise in providing decent, but mundane homes, was instead inspired architecture and town planning by the LCC Architects Department". *Anthony Tony Sargeant.*

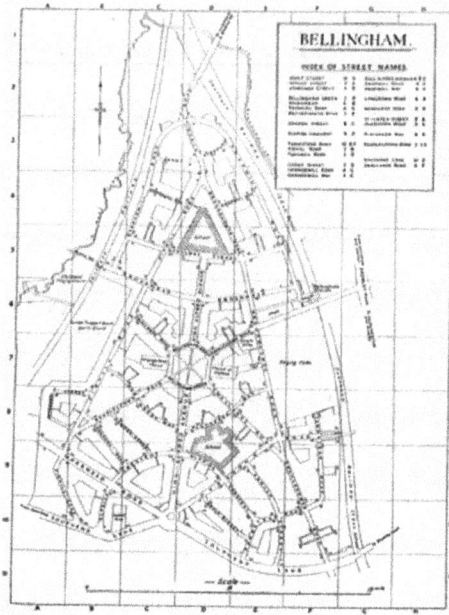

*The initial concept*

*Arial view as the estate takes shape*

*Under construction*

*The 'village' concept*

# Also by the Author

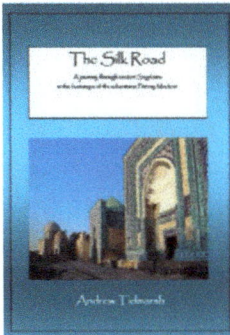

The Silk Road
A journey through
Sogdiana due for
release March 2026

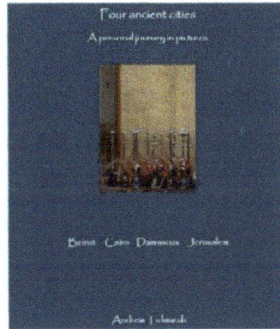

Four Ancient Cities
Cairo, Beirut, Damascus
Jerusalem due for release
summer 2026

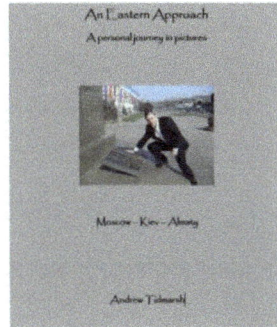

An eastern Approach
Moscow and beyond
due for release 2027

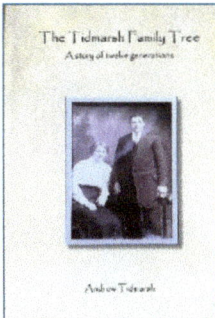

The Tidmarsh Family
Tree
A family history ISBN
978-1-80381-761-3

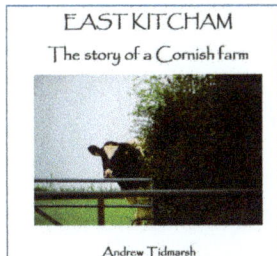

East Kitcham
The story of a Cornish
farm Due for release April
2026

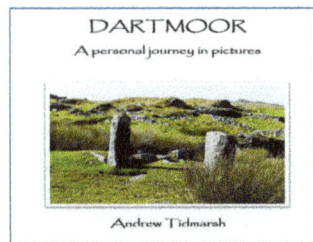

Dartmoor
A personal journey in pictures
Due for release March 2026